GREETINGS FROM ATTLEBORO
A HISTORICAL POSTCARD COLLECTION

By Shawn Viveiros

This collection would not have been possible without the invaluable support of the **Attleboro Historical Preservation Society**. Their dedication to preserving our shared history and their assistance in researching and cataloging these postcards has been instrumental. Thank you for helping bring this glimpse of Attleboro's past to life.

TABLE OF CONTENTS

Industry in Attleboro 3

Downtown Attleboro 16

Attleboro Courthouse 32

Attleboro Post Office 35

Attleboro Train Station 39

Streets of Attleboro 46

Homes of Attleboro 59

Attleboro's Hospital & Care 63

Attleboro Springs & Sanatorium 66

Attleboro Fire Station 75

Attleboro Public Library 78

Churches of Attleboro 82

National Shrine of Our Lady of La Salette 93

Attleboro Public Schools 98

Capron Park 108

Talaquega Park & Casino 115

Highland Country Club 121

Mechanics Pond 124

Monument Square 130

Miscellaneous Attleboro 135

A LETTER FROM THE AUTHOR

Welcome to "Greetings from Attleboro: A Historical Postcard Collection." Creating this book has been both a journey and a joy. Working alongside the Attleboro Historical Preservation Society organizing and implementing their new website, Attleboro.org, I have been captivated by the postcards within the collection—not only for their visual beauty but also for the stories they tell. This book emerged from a desire to preserve and share the vibrant history and evolving character of Attleboro through one of its most charming historical artifacts: postcards.

Each postcard in this collection offers a snapshot of our community's past, capturing moments from bustling streets and peaceful parks to thriving businesses and beloved homes. Equally compelling are the messages on their reverse sides, giving us poignant glimpses into the everyday lives, joys, and concerns of the people who lived here before us.

To fully appreciate this collection, I invite you to explore it in several ways:

Take your time. Each postcard is **a story in miniature**. Pause to consider both the image and its accompanying message. Due to space limitations, postcard transcriptions are not included here but can be found, along with additional content—including harder-to-read postcards—on Attleboro.org. Selected postcards within this book offer intriguing stories, enriched by additional context available online. I especially encourage you to explore the human touch evident in the handwritten notes.

Notice the **evolution of the town** through these images. They reveal Attleboro's growth, its changing architecture, fashions, and even transportation. Although most postcards date from 1900–1915, several predate this period, and a few more modern postcards are included. Many buildings and street names still exist today; you might recognize them immediately, while others may require a more discerning eye.

Reflect on the **personal connections** and emotional resonance within the written messages. These brief notes are often as illuminating as the pictures themselves. I have endeavored to include as many sent postcards as possible to showcase the sentiment of the time and reveal how residents of Attleboro and elsewhere viewed their world. This collection captures a variety of emotions, thoughts, and observations, which I encourage you to fully explore.

My hope is that this collection serves not only as a record of our past but also as a catalyst for conversation and memory-sharing within families and among friends. May it remind us all of the value of preserving local history and inspire future generations to cherish and document their own stories. Perhaps, just as we now look back 125 years at some of these postcards, this book itself might be rediscovered in another 125 years by future residents.

I hope you enjoy this collection,

SHAWN VIVIERIOS (Attleboro Resident)

PREFACE

POSTCARDS, AN EVOLUTION OF COMMUNICATION

In an age where communication is instantaneous, it is fascinating to reflect on how people once connected with one another over distances. The collection of postcards from Attleboro, spanning from the early 1900s to the 1970s, provides a window into a time when the postal service was a vital link between loved ones, friends, and acquaintances. These postcards, depicting various buildings, parks, and other notable locations in Attleboro, not only serve as historical artifacts but also offer a poignant reminder of the sentiments and challenges of communication in the past.

The story of the postcard begins in 1861, when the United States Congress passed an act allowing privately printed cards weighing one ounce or under to be sent through the mail. This seemingly small legislative change transformed the way people communicated. John P. Charlton secured the copyright for the first postcard in America that same year, laying the groundwork for what would become a revolutionary means of communication. This innovation came during a time of rapid transformation in the United States, as the Industrial Revolution reshaped American society. Factories were springing up, cities were expanding, and new technologies like the railroad and telegraph were making the vast distances of the United States feel smaller, connecting communities in unprecedented ways.

Before postcards, long-distance communication relied heavily on letters, which could be both cumbersome and costly. Sending a letter involved sealing it in an envelope, affixing a stamp, and waiting weeks for it to reach its destination. For many, the cost of postage was prohibitive, and the ability to send a quick note was simply out of reach. By 1898, Congress passed an act that allowed private printers to publish and sell cards to be posted at the 1-cent rate and stipulated the rules for printing postcards, including the wording to be used on the back of the cards. The introduction of picture postcards offered an affordable, straightforward alternative—just a card with space for a message on one side and the recipient's address on the other. This simplicity, combined with their low cost, democratized communication and made it accessible to people from all walks of life.

The reliance on postcards highlights the role of the postal service as a lifeline for communication during this era. Travel at the time was fraught with challenges, and journeys could be uncertain. A simple message like "We arrived safely" carried profound significance, offering reassurance to loved ones waiting at home. Today, we might say "text me when you get home," underscoring our desire for instant reassurance. In the early 1900s, however, that reassurance came through the slower medium of postcards, reflecting both the limitations and the ingenuity of the time.

Postcards also coincided with a growing interest in visual culture. Advances in printing technology made it possible to mass-produce high-quality, colorful postcards, while the rise of photography allowed people to see images of far-off places and important landmarks. Picture postcards became immensely popular, and Attleboro, with its charming streets and notable landmarks, was frequently featured. These postcards offered not only written messages but also visual snapshots of the town, creating a rich tapestry of social history that captures the essence of local businesses, churches, schools, parks, and streets across different decades. As the town grew and changed in the early twentieth century, postcards documented its transformation. The postcards featured in this collection capture unique moments in time, offering a window into the everyday lives of Attleboro's residents. They show us bustling streets, thriving businesses, and beautiful parks, and more importantly, they show us the people of Attleboro—their hopes, their dreams, and their desire to stay connected with one another.

As the twentieth century progressed, the popularity of postcards continued to grow as the "Golden Era of Postcards" was ushered in from 1901 through 1915. However, the invention of the telephone and other consumer technologies began to change the landscape of communication. By the 1920s, the ability to make a phone call offered a quicker way to connect, leading to a gradual decline in the number of postcards sent. The last significant postcard era, known as the "chrome" era, began around 1939 and became dominant in the 1950s, despite initial challenges during World War II due to material shortages; with a steady decline into the modern era.

The Attleboro postcard collection offers more than just a glimpse into the past; it invites us to reflect on the evolution of communication and our ongoing desire to stay connected. This collection, "Greetings from Attleboro: A Historical Postcard Collection," invites you to step back in time to a world of handwritten notes, unique Attleboro landmarks, and bustling streets and commons. This book is more than just a collection of postcards; it is a journey through time, capturing the essence of Attleboro and illustrating the remarkable journey of human communication with handwritten notes from residences. Each page invites you to connect with the past and experience the pride, warmth, and sense of community that has always defined Attleboro. As you explore these postcards, may you feel the enduring connection that bridges generations and be reminded of the stories that make Attleboro truly special.

https://siarchives.si.edu/history/featured-topics/postcard/postcard-history

Industry in Attleboro

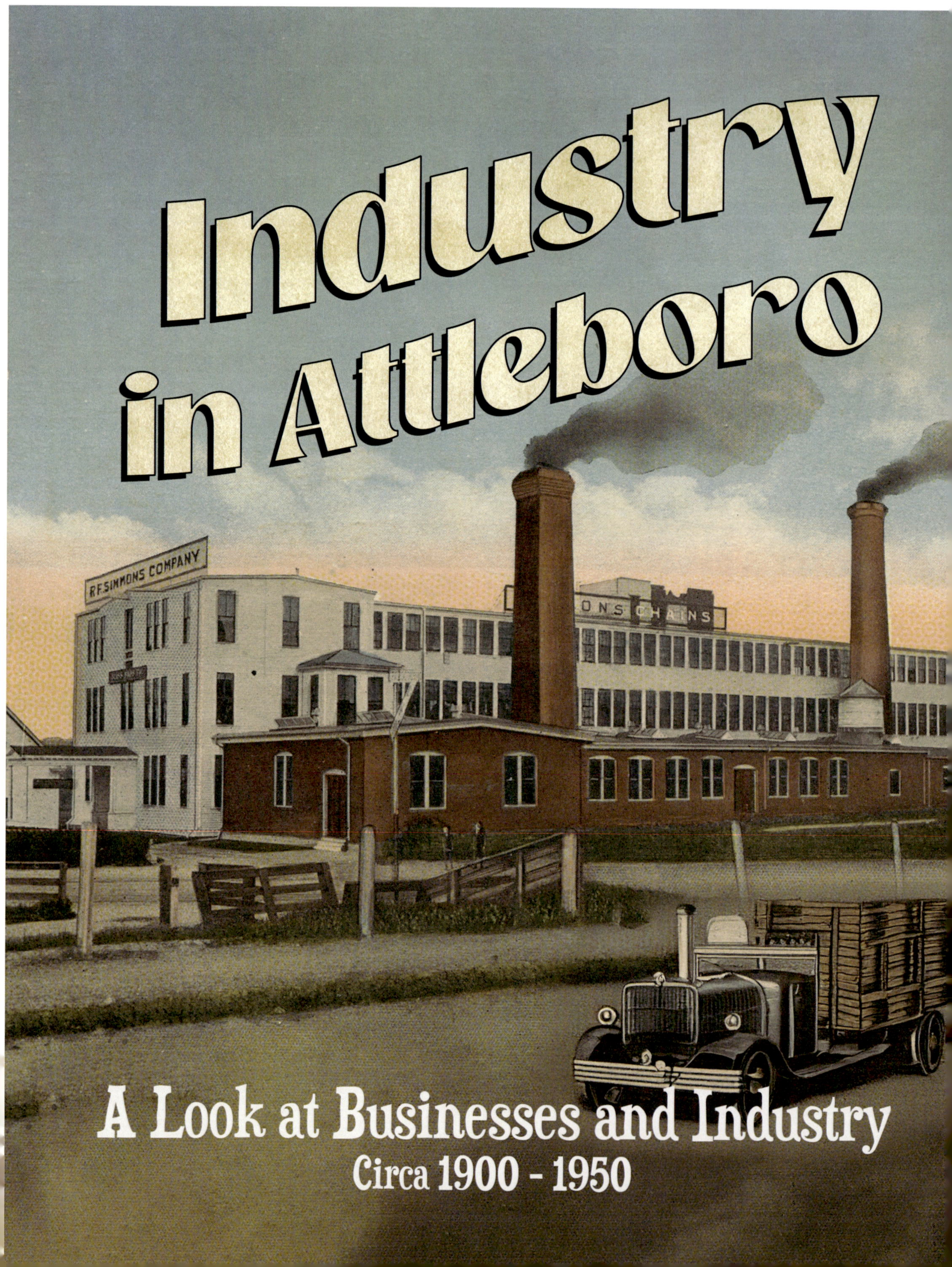

A Look at Businesses and Industry
Circa 1900 - 1950

INDUSTRY IN ATTLEBORO

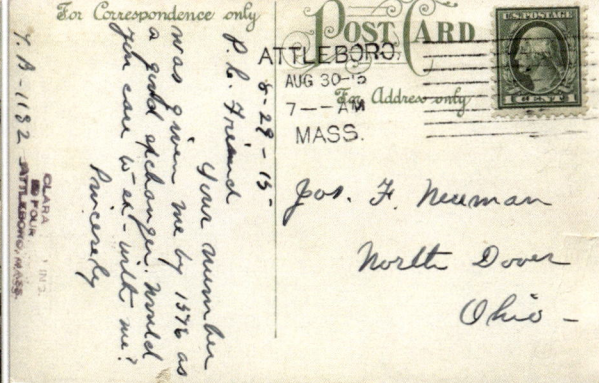

The **James E. Blake Co.**, founded in 1881 in Attleboro, Massachusetts, was a key player in the city's thriving jewelry industry. Originally known as Blake & Caflin, it was later incorporated in 1898. Before focusing on sterling and silver-plated novelty items, vanity pieces, and tableware, the company gained recognition for producing Civil War military insignia. Operating during the golden age of Attleboro's manufacturing boom, the James E. Blake Co. contributed significantly to the local economy. Known for its craftsmanship and innovation, the company employed 75 operatives and maintained a capital of $100,000 before ceasing operations in the late 1930s, leaving a lasting legacy in silverware design.

The **Bliss Bros. Co.**, founded in 1896 in Attleboro, Massachusetts, was a prominent jewelry manufacturer. Originally known as Bliss Brothers & Everett, the company produced a wide range of products, including lockets, hinged bangle bracelets, and interpretations of Austro-Hungarian designs. Using karat gold, sterling silver, and gold-filled metals, they introduced notable product lines such as the "Colonial Dame" series and patented "Surefit" watchbands. By the early 20th century, Bliss Bros. employed 60 operatives and became synonymous with craftsmanship and creativity. The company remained a significant contributor to Attleboro's jewelry heritage before ceasing operations in the mid-20th century.

The **R.F. Simmons Co.**, founded in 1873 by Robert Fitz Simmons, was a pioneering jewelry manufacturer in Attleboro, Massachusetts. Known for its high-quality watch chains, lockets, and bracelets, the company introduced innovations like chain catalogs in 1881 and safety fasteners for chains in the 1890s. Employing over 250 workers by the late 19th century, Simmons products bore trademarks such as "Armilla" and "Betsy Ross." Their adaptability and reach extended to international offices, solidifying the company's role in making Attleboro a global jewelry hub.

The **Watson & Newell Company**, established in 1880, became a leading name in Attleboro's sterling silver industry. Starting as Cobb, Gould & Co. in 1874, it evolved through several iterations before becoming The Watson Co. in 1920. Located at a historic factory on Mechanic Street, the company employed over 200 workers at its peak and produced sterling flatware, souvenir spoons, and vanity items. Their holloware designs for Wilcox & Wagoner in the early 1900s expanded their reputation. Acquired by R. Wallace & Sons in 1955, the factory was later listed on the National Register of Historic Places in 2020.

GREETINGS FROM ATTLEBORO

BATES BUILDING NO. 1, ATTLEBORO, MASS. PUBLISHED FOR S. P. CLARK & CO.

The Bates Building, showing the Railroad Centre, and other Manufacturing Buildings, Attleboro, Mass.

Published for S. P. Clark & Co.

INDUSTRY IN ATTLEBORO

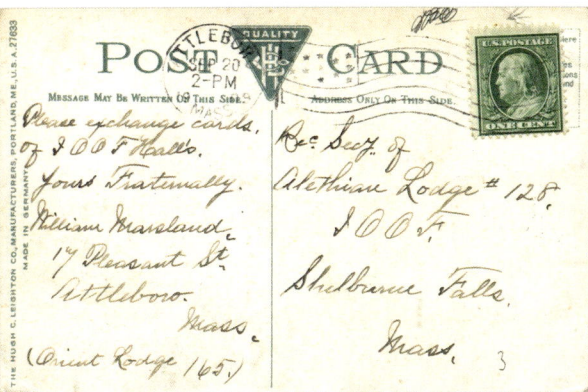

S.O. Bigney & Co., established in 1879 as Marsh & Bigney, became a standalone entity in 1894 under Samuel O. Bigney's leadership. By 1907, the company was among the largest jewelry manufacturers in the U.S., employing 100 operatives and producing gold-filled chains and novelties. Known for his fair labor practices, Bigney paid women $2 per day and men $3, far above average wages. His motto, "Eternal hustle coupled with honesty and integrity is the just price of success," defined his approach. Bigney also played a prominent role in politics, serving on the Governor's Council and attending national conventions.

The **Holiday Inn South Attleboro** opened in 1962 along Route 95, serving travelers with 120 units and a restaurant. A key rest stop for three decades, the hotel played a vital role in the region's hospitality industry before being redeveloped into a shopping plaza in the 1990s.

GREETINGS FROM ATTLEBORO

Attleboro Manufacturing Co., Attleboro, Mass.

Attleboro, Mass. The R. F. Simmons Company Building.

Webster Co., Attleboro, Mass.

Pub. by A. R. Block

INDUSTRY IN ATTLEBORO

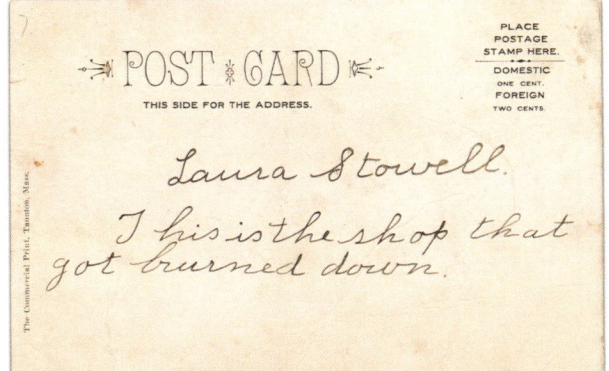

The **Attleboro Manufacturing Company,** founded in the late 1890s by Samuel Stone and Maurice Baer, became a leader in both women's and men's jewelry. After a fire destroyed their original facility, the company rebuilt and launched the successful "Baer and Wilde" division in 1908. Their innovative "Kum-A-Part" cuff button gained national acclaim in 1918. During World War I, the company produced military identification tags, transitioning to men's accessories post-war. Rebranded as Swank, Inc. in 1941, it became one of the most recognized names in men's fashion accessories throughout the 20th century.

The **Leach & Garner Company,** established in 1899, played a vital role in the precious metals industry in Attleboro. Founded by Edwin F. Leach at 23, the company initially focused on jewelry findings like clasps and beads. By the early 20th century, it employed 100 operatives and manufactured gold and silver plate materials in sheet, wire, and tube forms. Over time, they diversified into government markets and advanced materials. In 2013, Leach & Garner became part of the Richline Group, further solidifying their legacy in innovation and precious metals.

W.H. Wilmarth & Co., founded in the 1860s, epitomized Attleboro's transition to industrial-scale jewelry manufacturing. Originally a partnership known as Bronson & Wilmarth, it later specialized in casket and coffin trimmings. By 1890, the company was a major employer and innovator in refining techniques, helping to establish Attleboro as "Jewelrydom." Its contribution to industrial growth showcased the city's shift from small artisan shops to large-scale factories.

The Webster Company, founded as G.K. Webster & Co. in 1869 by George K. Webster, was a leading manufacturer of sterling silver products in North Attleboro. Their hallmark—"W" with a feathered arrow—was synonymous with quality in flatware, napkin rings, and candlesticks. Acquired by Reed & Barton in 1950, the Webster Company continued operating independently until its original building was demolished in 2015, marking the end of an era in silver craftsmanship.

*Artists Interpretation

GREETINGS FROM ATTLEBORO

Attleboro, Mass. The S. O. Bigney Building.
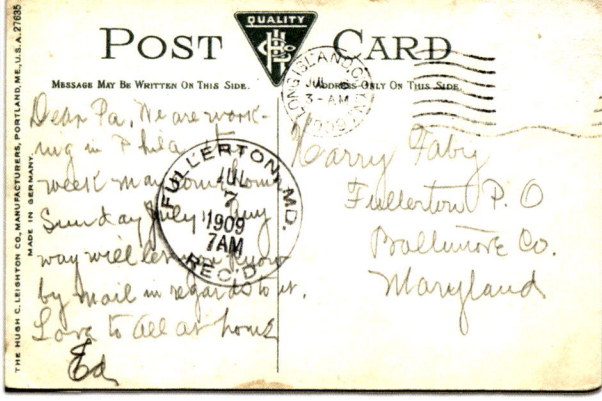

Attleboro, Mass. The Old Shuttle Factory.
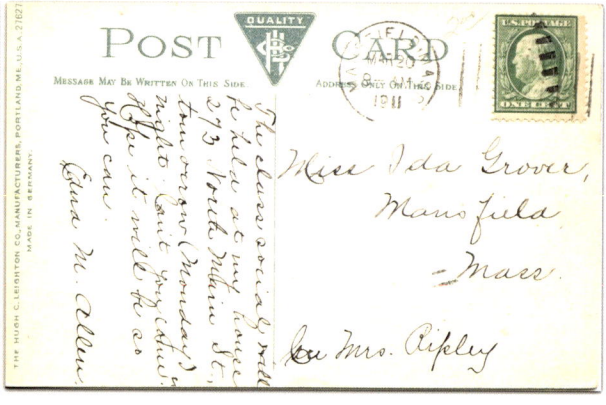

Watson & Newell Factory. Attleboro, Mass.
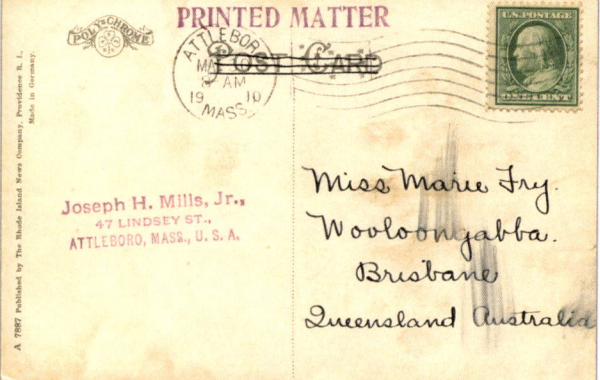

INDUSTRY IN ATTLEBORO

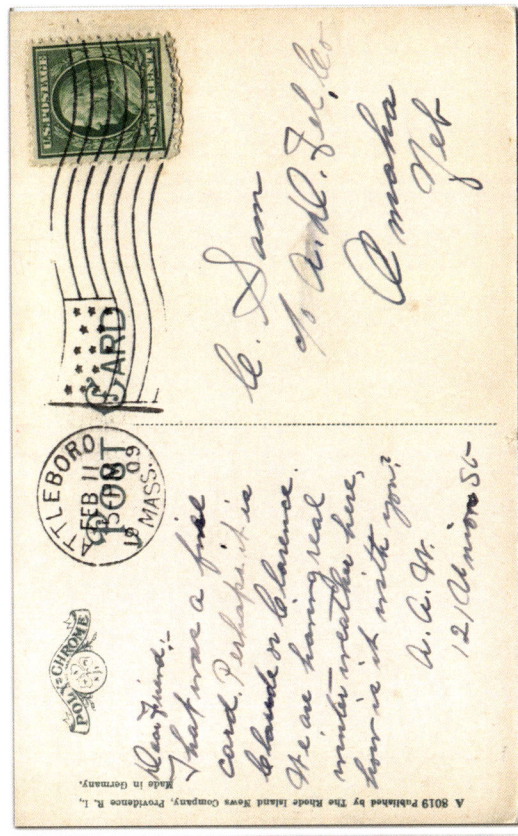

A Snapshot of Winter 1909

On February 11, 1909, a postcard was sent from Attleboro, Massachusetts, with the sender remarking, **"We are having real winter weather here."** This simple yet evocative statement hints at the broader context of that winter, which was marked by significant snowstorms across the United States. This postcard was addressed to Omaha, Nebraska, a city that, ironically, had endured even harsher conditions just days prior.

The winter weather referred to may well have been the remnants of a powerful storm system that struck Sioux Falls, South Dakota, on February 8 and 9. This storm, one of the largest on record for the region, began on a Monday afternoon and continued until early Wednesday morning. Sioux Falls recorded an astounding 21 inches of snow, accompanied by high winds that created massive drifts. The impact was severe, with rail lines across the Midwest, including those connecting to Omaha, disrupted by the storm's ferocity.

By the time this weather system traveled eastward, it likely diminished in intensity but still delivered enough snowfall and cold to leave an impression on Attleboro residents. This period in history predates modern weather forecasting and infrastructure, meaning communities relied heavily on written correspondence, newspapers, and local observations to stay informed about the weather. Such conditions often heightened the isolation caused by storms, as travel and communication were frequently disrupted.

This particular postcard serves as a vivid reminder of how people in the early 20th century coped with the unpredictability of winter. It also highlights the importance of postal services as a lifeline for sharing news and maintaining connections, even in adverse weather. The fact that this card made its way to Omaha, despite the recent storm closures, is a tcapturing the determination of the postal workers of the time.

In today's context, it's fascinating to consider how a simple postcard can encapsulate a moment in history. Through this brief message, we glimpse not only the challenges of winter in 1909 but also the resilience of communities in the face of nature's power.

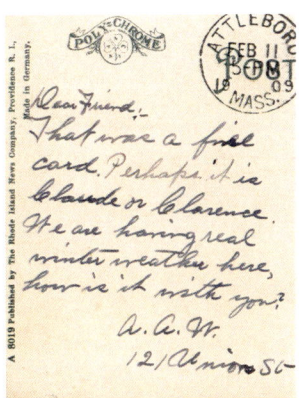

Dear Friend,

That was a fine card. Perhaps it is Claude or Clarence. We are having real winter weather here, how is it with you?

A.A.W.
12 Union St.

S.O. Bigney & Co.
A Jewel in Attleboro's Industrial Crown

In 1906, a postcard sent from Attleboro, Massachusetts, boldly declared the town as the *"jewelry center of America."* This message, penned with unmistakable pride, highlighted the work of "first-class artisans in silver and gold chains, bracelets, lockets, etc." Among the many treasures crafted in Attleboro's bustling workshops, the postcard singled out the *"celebrated Bigney chain,"* a product of S.O. Bigney & Co., one of the city's prominent jewelry manufacturers.

The Bigney chain was more than just a product—it was a symbol of Attleboro's mastery in jewelry craftsmanship. S.O. Bigney & Co., established in 1896, was known for producing high-quality gold-filled chains, watch straps, and bracelets. The company operated at the cutting edge of its time, utilizing patented processes and innovative designs to distinguish itself from competitors. Bigney's products, including its patented "Square Corner" and "Boston Link" chains, were highly sought after for their durability and elegance, making them ideal for both business and formal occasions.

The company's attention to detail and innovation set it apart in the competitive world of jewelry manufacturing. A 1928 catalog from Bigney highlights their patented designs, including the "U-WAN-A" and "STA-SNUG" watch straps, which were lauded for their comfort and durability. The company also emphasized its exclusive "Persian Inlay" technique, protected under a 1922 patent, which allowed for intricate color treatments on metal surfaces. These advancements ensured that Bigney's products were not only functional but visually stunning, reflecting the artistry of the craftsmen who created them.

Attleboro's prominence in the jewelry world extended far beyond S.O. Bigney & Co. The town was home to numerous manufacturers whose work collectively earned it the title of "jewelry center of America." Companies like Robbins Co., Whiting & Davis, and D.E. Makepeace Co. contributed to the area's thriving economy and reputation for excellence. Together, these manufacturers formed the backbone of a community defined by its dedication to quality and craftsmanship.

The postcard featuring S.O. Bigney's celebrated chain serves as a snapshot of a golden era in Attleboro's history. It provides a glimpse into the pride and ingenuity that characterized the town's jewelry industry in the early 20th century. Today, the legacy of S.O. Bigney & Co. endures through the antique chains, bracelets, and watch straps that remain prized by collectors and historians alike. These artifacts stand as a testament to the skill and innovation that once made Attleboro shine as a beacon of American manufacturing.

With its focus on artistry, technical innovation, and commitment to excellence, S.O. Bigney & Co. played a vital role in shaping the identity of Attleboro and its place in the annals of industrial history. This story, preserved through the postcard and other historical records, offers a fascinating look at a time when the city truly was the jewelry capital of America.

INDUSTRY IN ATTLEBORO

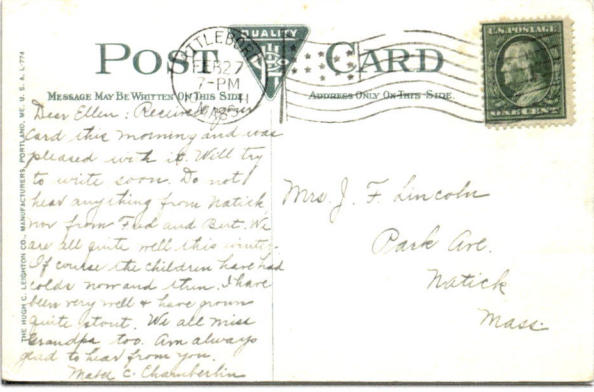

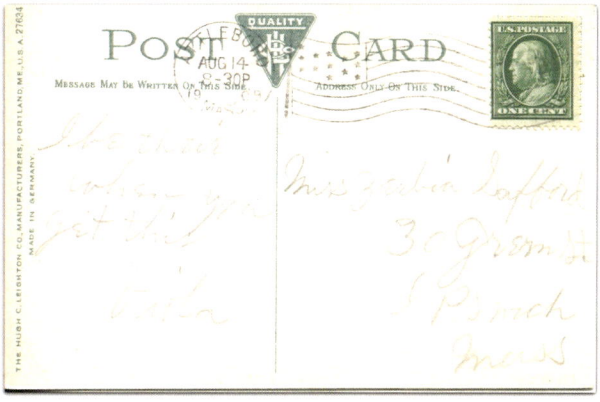

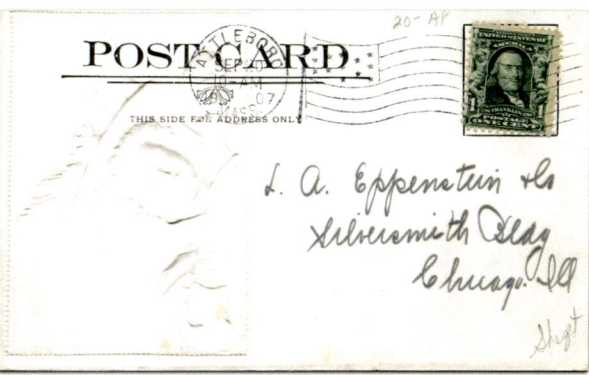

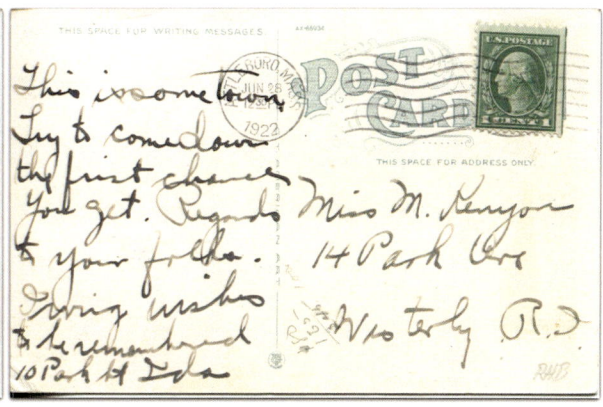

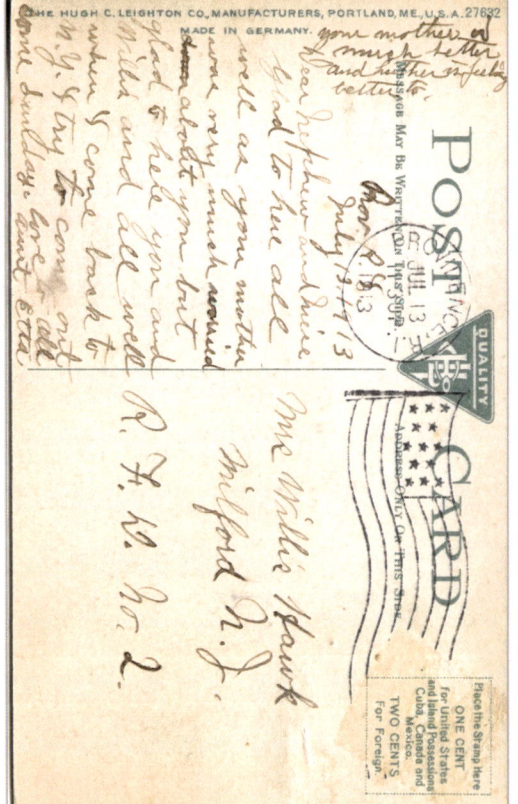

INDUSTRY IN ATTLEBORO

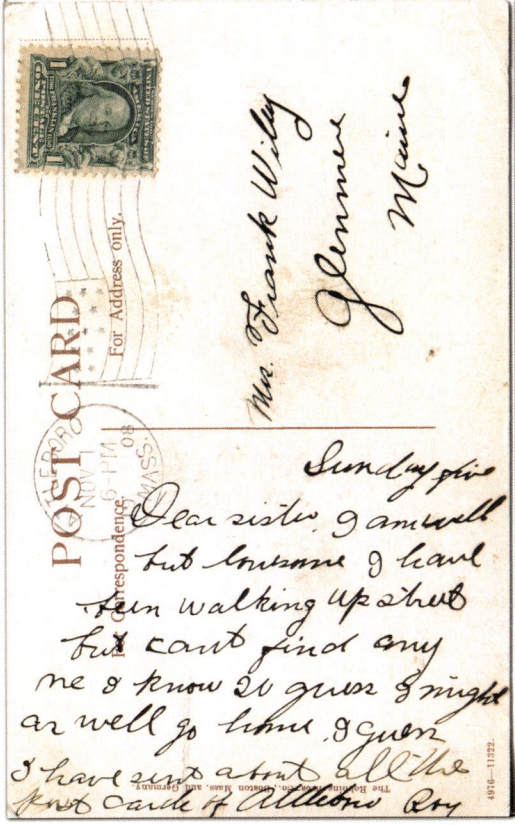

Connections Across Distances: Postcards as a Window into Early 20th-Century Attleboro

The postcards of early 20th-century Attleboro reveal the rich tapestry of relationships and emotions that defined life in this era. Whether fostering friendships, maintaining family bonds, or navigating moments of solitude, these handwritten messages served as vital threads connecting people across distances.

In 1911, Ernest Hallett received a postcard; *seen on the previous page,* from a friend who inquired about his progress in school and shared news from another friend, Melda. This exchange highlights how education was not only a personal milestone but also a shared value within the community. Friends encouraged each other's growth and celebrated achievements, fostering a culture of mutual support. In an era when communication required time and effort, such thoughtful correspondence underscored the deep importance placed on maintaining friendships.

The postcard sent in 1913 by Aunt Etta; *seen on the previous page,* to her nephew and niece offers a heartfelt glimpse into the care and concern that defined familial relationships. She reassured them that their parents' health was improving and expressed her relief at their well-being. Her words also conveyed her intention to visit once she returned from New York, emphasizing the lengths families went to maintain connections despite physical separation. These messages were more than updates; they were tokens of love and a reminder that even across miles, family was a source of strength and comfort.

Not all postcards were filled with joy. In 1908, Ray sent a postcard; seen *on this page,* to his sister, candidly sharing his loneliness as he wandered Attleboro's streets without finding familiar faces. Despite his feelings, Ray mentioned that he had been sending many postcards of the town, reflecting the effort people made to remain connected. His vulnerability offers an introspective look at the quieter moments of life in Attleboro, where even bustling streets could feel isolating.

Together, these postcards paint a vivid picture of early 20th-century Attleboro, where handwritten notes served as lifelines that carried not just news, but also emotions, care, and resilience. They highlight a community rooted in the values of education, family, and emotional connection, reminding us that even in an industrializing world, the most meaningful connections were deeply personal. These small, everyday acts of communication helped weave the social fabric of Attleboro, preserving moments of love, longing, and shared humanity for generations to come.

GREETINGS FROM ATTLEBORO

The Expressmen's Strike of 1910 and Its Impact on Attleboro

In October of 1910, a significant labor strike erupted in New York City, known as the Expressmen's Strike. This pivotal moment in labor history not only disrupted commerce in one of the nation's largest cities but also sent ripples through industrial towns like Attleboro, Massachusetts. For many Attleboro residents, particularly those employed in the bustling jewelry manufacturing sector, the strike underscored the fragile nature of labor and business during the early 20th century.

The Expressmen's Strike was led by workers employed by major express companies, who handled freight and packages critical to the operation of businesses across the country. The strike arose from grievances about poor wages, unsafe working conditions, and the companies' refusal to recognize workers' unions. Elisabeth Gurley Flynn, a prominent labor activist, described the strike in a December 1910 article for the International Socialist Review, highlighting the courage and resilience of the workers as they stood against powerful corporate interests.

While centered in New York, the strike's impact was far-reaching. Disruptions to the transport of goods and raw materials created uncertainty for businesses dependent on timely shipments. Factories in smaller towns like Attleboro, which relied on the steady flow of materials for production, were not immune to these effects. Workers and business owners alike faced anxiety about how long the strike might last and whether it would destabilize their livelihoods.

In 1910, Attleboro was thriving as a hub for jewelry manufacturing. The town's factories produced high-quality items that were distributed throughout the country. However, the prosperity of Attleboro's workforce was precarious, tethered to national supply chains and labor dynamics.

The Postcard, sent on October 31, 1910, provides a poignant snapshot of life during this time. The message, penned by F.E. Stearns, reflects both the pride and the uncertainty felt by workers. Writing to Capt. J.E. Archibald in Port Clyde, Maine, Stearns notes the strike in New York and its potential implications for his work: *"There is a big strike in New York. I don't know how long business will last."* His words convey a sense of apprehension, tempered by a dedication to his craft and a longing for connection.

The feelings expressed in Stearns' postcard were likely shared by many Attleboro residents. While strikes like the one in New York were a testament to the growing strength of organized labor, they also highlighted the vulnerability of workers whose jobs depended on stable economic conditions. For factory workers in Attleboro, the possibility of supply chain disruptions threatened not just their immediate income but their ability to sustain their families. The early 20th century was a transformative period for labor in the United States. The Expressmen's Strike of 1910 exemplified the growing tension between workers and industrialists. Attleboro's response to such events reflects the complexity of life in a factory town. While workers were acutely aware of their dependence on the smooth operation of national supply chains, many also yearned for greater fairness and stability in their own lives.

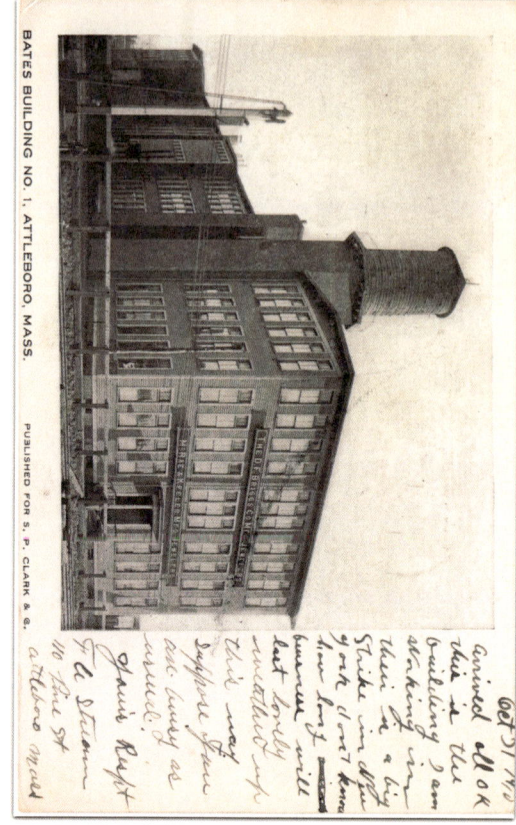

GREETINGS FROM ATTLEBORO

DOWNTOWN ATTLEBORO

Park Street, Attleboro, Mass.

Park Street, looking west. Bronson Building in the distance. Attleboro, Mass.
Photo by H. T. Bates, Attleboro

PARK STREET, ATTLEBORO, MASSACHUSETTS 1403

GREETINGS FROM ATTLEBORO

DOWNTOWN ATTLEBORO

From Electric Cars to Automobiles: Attleboro's Evolving Streetscape

In the early 20th century, Attleboro was a town bustling with bicycles and the occasional electric streetcar. The streets were narrow, designed for pedestrians, horse-drawn carriages, and the efficient electric trolleys that once wove through the town center. However, the dawn of the automobile era brought significant changes to both transportation and urban planning.

One of the clearest examples of this shift can be seen through historical photographs taken from nearly the same perspective, decades apart. In the earlier image, an electric car and bicycles dominate the road, a scene reminiscent of a time when public transit was the primary mode of urban mobility. The later image, taken approximately 30 to 40 years later, reveals a stark contrast—wider streets, automobiles replacing bicycles, and an overall transformation of Attleboro's infrastructure to accommodate the needs of modern vehicles.

The introduction of the automobile to Attleboro, like many other American towns, was met with both excitement and challenges. At first, cars were a luxury, owned by only a few, but as mass production reduced costs, they became more common. The growing popularity of automobiles meant that roads originally built for trolleys and pedestrians had to be expanded. Attleboro took a significant step in this transition by widening its streets by 15 feet—a clear indicator of how crucial automobiles had become to daily life.

This expansion had profound effects on the town. It allowed for increased traffic flow and encouraged commercial development along major roads. The widened streets provided space for parking, allowing businesses to attract more customers arriving by car rather than on foot or by trolley. However, this shift also signaled the decline of electric streetcars, which gradually disappeared as personal vehicles took over.

Beyond infrastructure, the cultural impact of the automobile was just as transformative. The freedom to travel farther and faster reshaped how people lived and worked. Commuting became more practical, leading to the growth of suburban areas around Attleboro. Meanwhile, the need for gas stations, repair shops, and dealerships created entirely new industries within the town.

DOWNTOWN ATTLEBORO

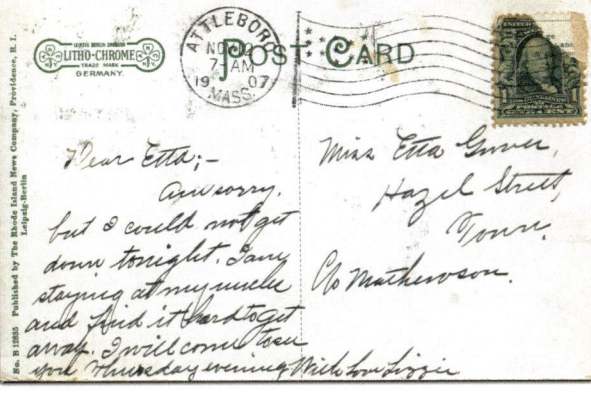

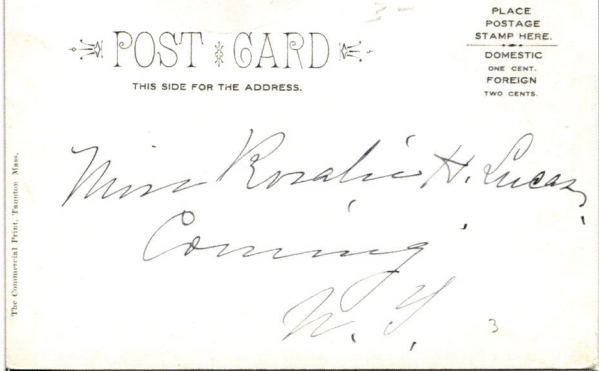

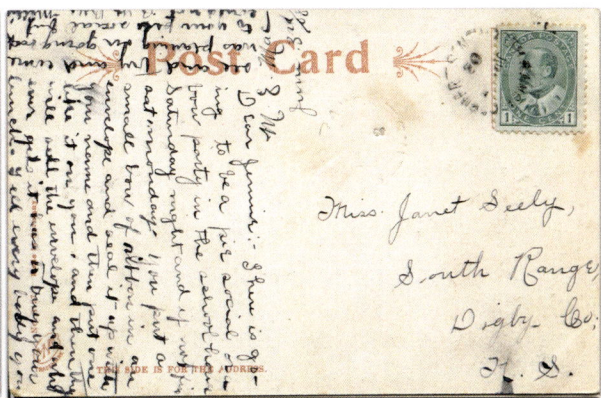

GREETINGS FROM ATTLEBORO

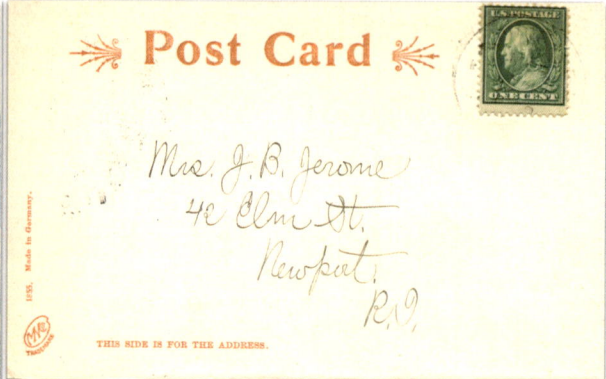

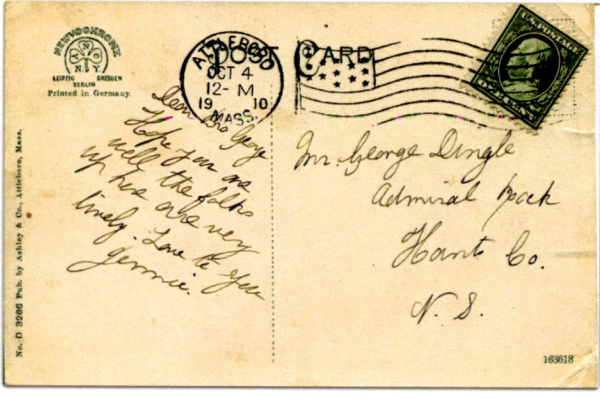

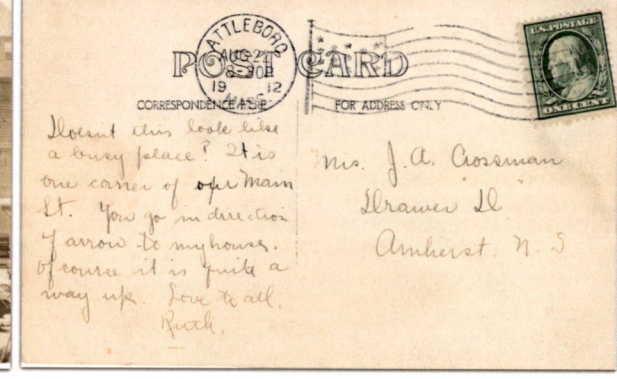

DOWNTOWN ATTLEBORO

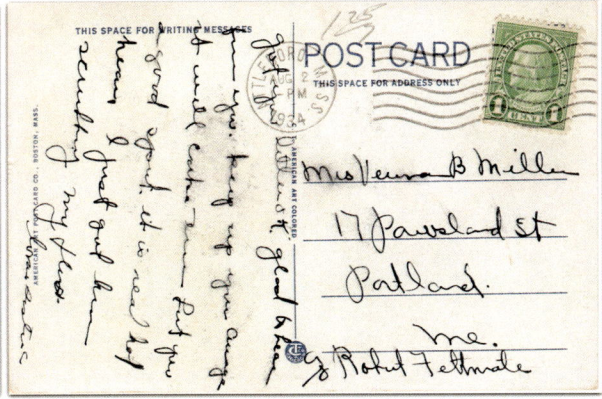

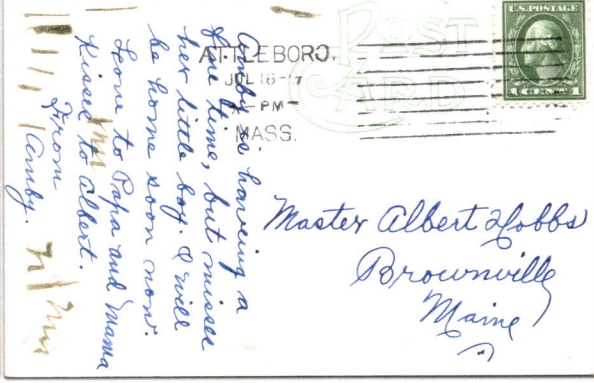

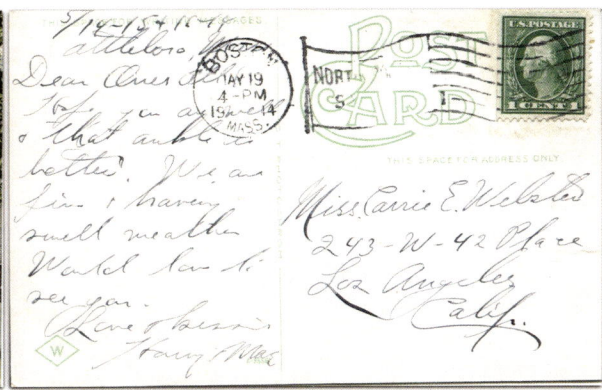

GREETINGS FROM ATTLEBORO

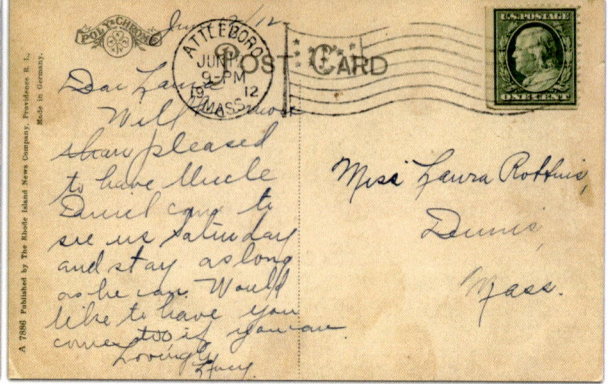

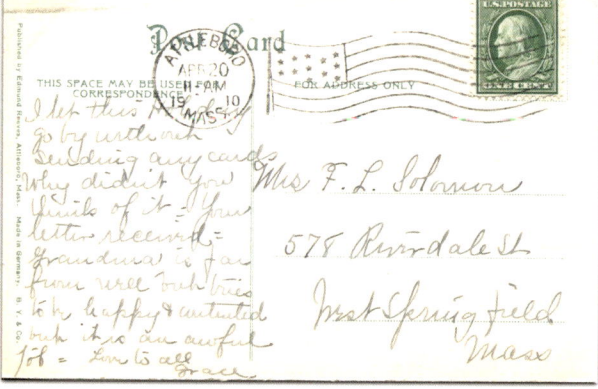

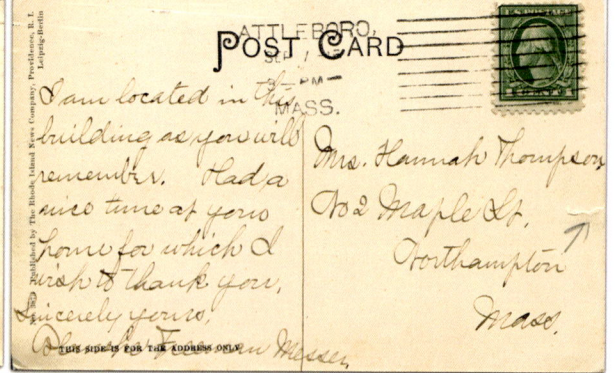

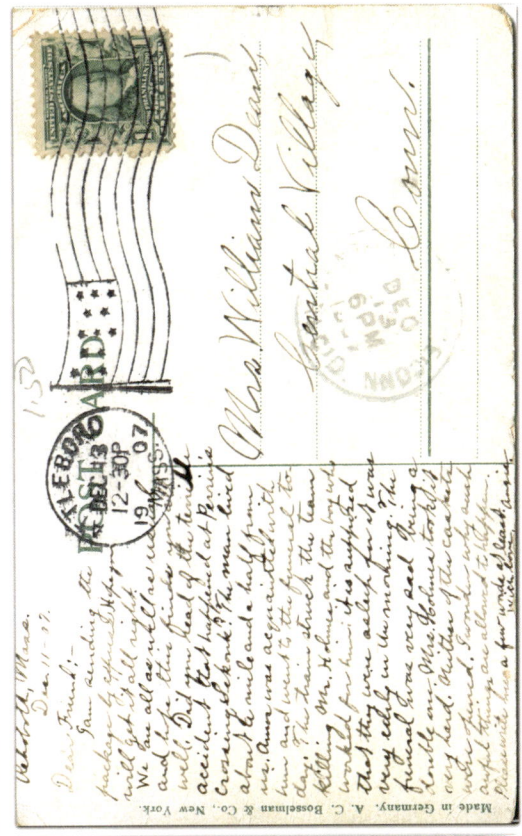

Perrin's Crossing Tragedy: A Community Mourns

On December 10, 1907, a devastating accident at Perrin's Crossing in Seekonk tragically ended the lives of Edward J. Holmes, a 45-year-old Rehoboth milk dealer, and his 18-year-old assistant, Clarence Brown. The men were on their routine morning delivery to Pawtucket when their milk wagon was struck by freight train 976 in the early hours. It is believed they had fallen asleep during the journey. Despite the train crew's efforts to signal with warning whistles, the wagon was destroyed upon impact, killing both men instantly. The horse pulling the wagon miraculously survived and was later found unharmed nearby.

An inquest ruled out negligence on the part of the train crew, confirming that all precautions, including the ringing of the train's bell, had been taken. Nevertheless, the incident underscored the dangers posed by railroads, especially at crossings like Perrin's, which were gated but still hazardous, particularly in low visibility or quiet hours.

The double funeral, held on December 12, 1907, deeply affected the community. Edward J. Holmes was a well-known figure, operating a successful farm and milk delivery business, and Clarence Brown, though less established, had become well-liked in the area. The writer of a contemporaneous postcard, likely a neighbor of Holmes, offered a first-hand account of attending the solemn event: *"The train struck the team killing Mr. Holmes and the boy who worked for him... The funeral was very sad. Being a double one. Mrs. Holmes took it very hard. Neither of the caskets were opened. I wonder why such awful things are allowed to happen."*

This poignant message, sent to a Mrs. William Deans in Connecticut, not only conveyed the heartbreak of the moment but also captured a broader sense of helplessness shared by many who encountered such sudden tragedies in the early 20th century.

The accident reflects a period of significant transformation in American society. Railroads, essential for economic growth and connectivity, also brought new risks to rural communities unaccustomed to such powerful infrastructure. The collision at Perrin's Crossing serves as a sobering reminder of these dangers and the profound impact they had on the lives of everyday people.

Through the lens of this postcard and the events it recounts, we gain insight into the fragility of life in this era and the resilience of communities like Attleboro, Rehoboth and Seekonk, who came together to mourn and support one another in the face of loss. The writer's closing reflection—"I wonder why such awful things are allowed to happen"—resonates as a timeless sentiment, connecting us to the human struggles of over a century ago.

The Attleboro Sun, Vol, XIX., No. 56 Tuesday, December 10, 1907
The Attleboro Sun, Vol. XIX., No. 57 Wednesday, December 11, 1907
The Attleboro Sun, Monday, December 30, 1907

GREETINGS FROM ATTLEBORO

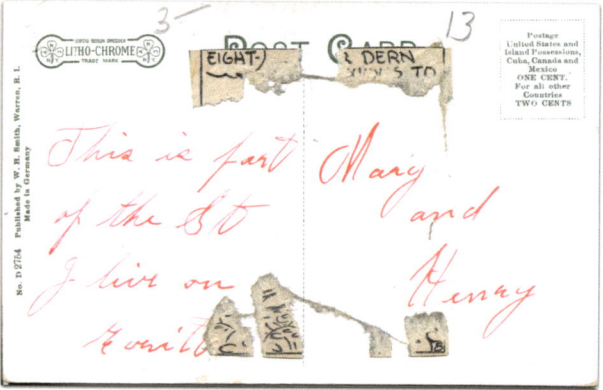

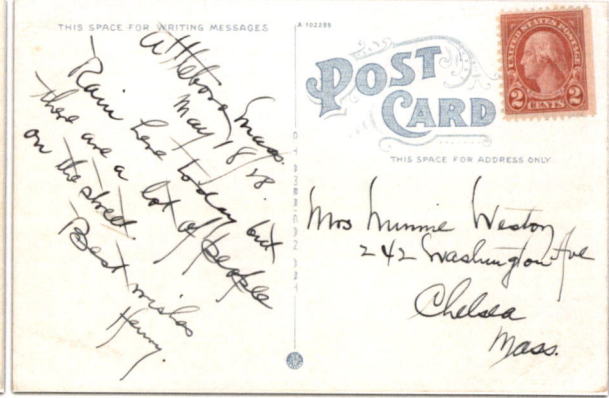

NORTH MAIN STREET FROM PARK ST., ATTLEBORO, MASS.

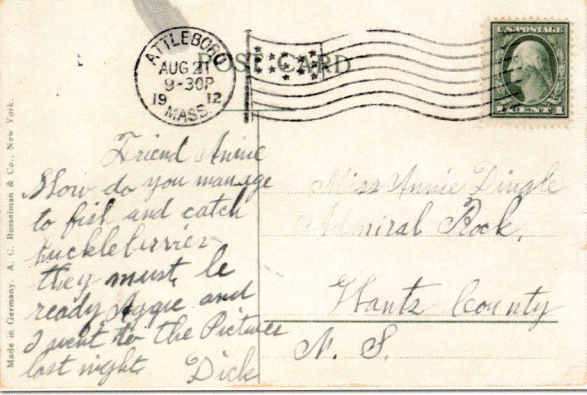

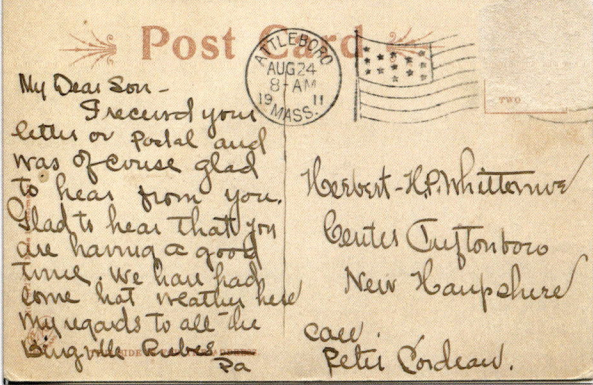

GREETINGS FROM ATTLEBORO

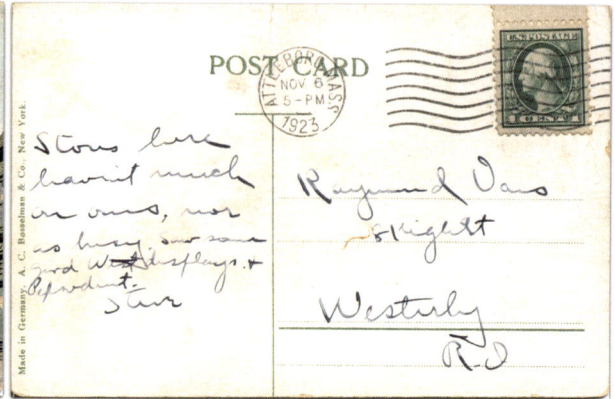

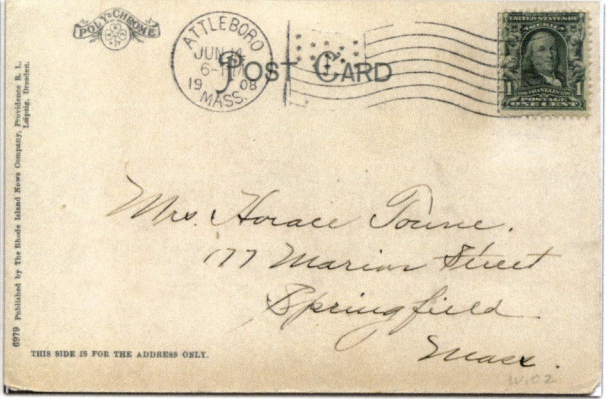

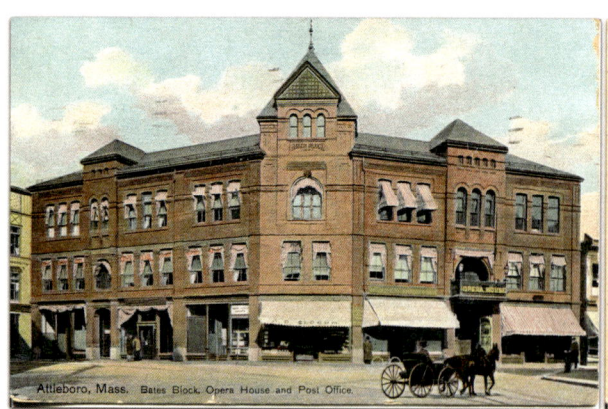
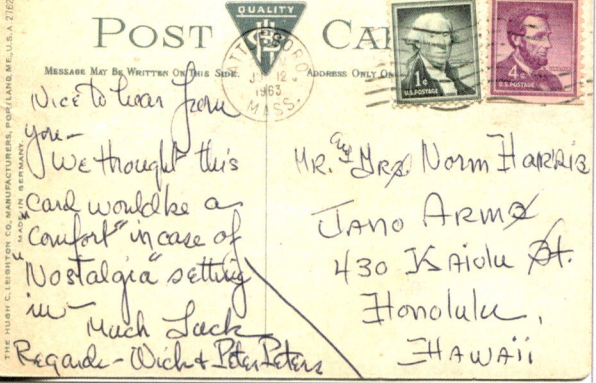

DOWNTOWN ATTLEBORO

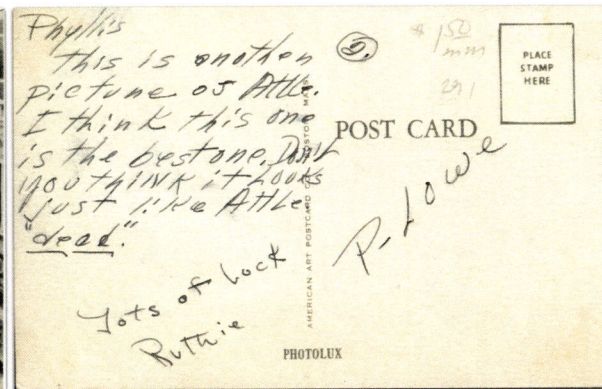

Reflections from Ruthie: A Personal Connection to Attleboro

From these postcards, a unique glimpse into the relationship between Ruthie and Phyllis, two correspondents bound by shared memories and a humorous, if slightly melancholic, perspective on Attleboro. Ruthie's messages, filled with wit and subtle nostalgia, transform the postcards into more than mere correspondence—they become snapshots of an emotional landscape shaped by their experiences.

As seen from the top postcard, Ruthie reminds Phyllis of their Wednesday night walks down a particular street. Her description of Attleboro as an **"awful place"**; shown with a black drawn arrow seen centered on the image, is softened by the tender act of remembering shared moments, showing that even in critique, there is affection. The simplicity of her address to "P. Lowe" adds a layer of intimacy, as though the intended recipient needs no further identification.

The bottom postcard continues this interplay of humor and sentiment. Ruthie compares the image on the card to a **"dead"** Attleboro, perhaps a playful jab at the town's quiet or uneventful nature. Despite this, her choice to share **"another picture of Attle"** suggests an unspoken fondness or, at the very least, a shared understanding of the place's significance in their lives.

These postcards stand as reminders that history is not only about grand events or well-documented landmarks but also about the everyday connections between people. Ruthie and Phyllis's correspondence illustrates how Attleboro—whether seen as "awful" or "dead"—was a backdrop to their friendship. The humor in their observations adds a human touch to our understanding of the town, reminding us that places are often defined as much by their emotional resonance as by their physical attributes.

Artist depiction of Ruthie and Phyllis

GREETINGS FROM ATTLEBORO

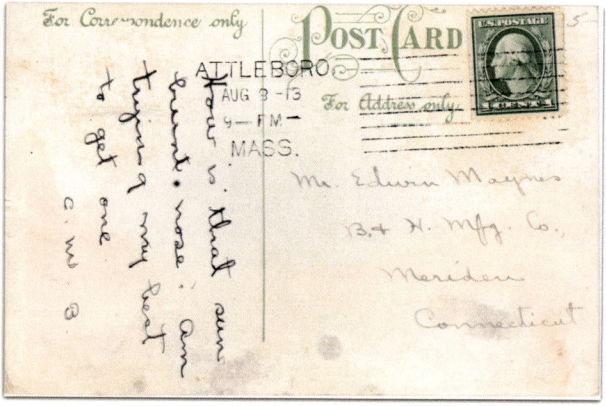

Attleboro Courthouse

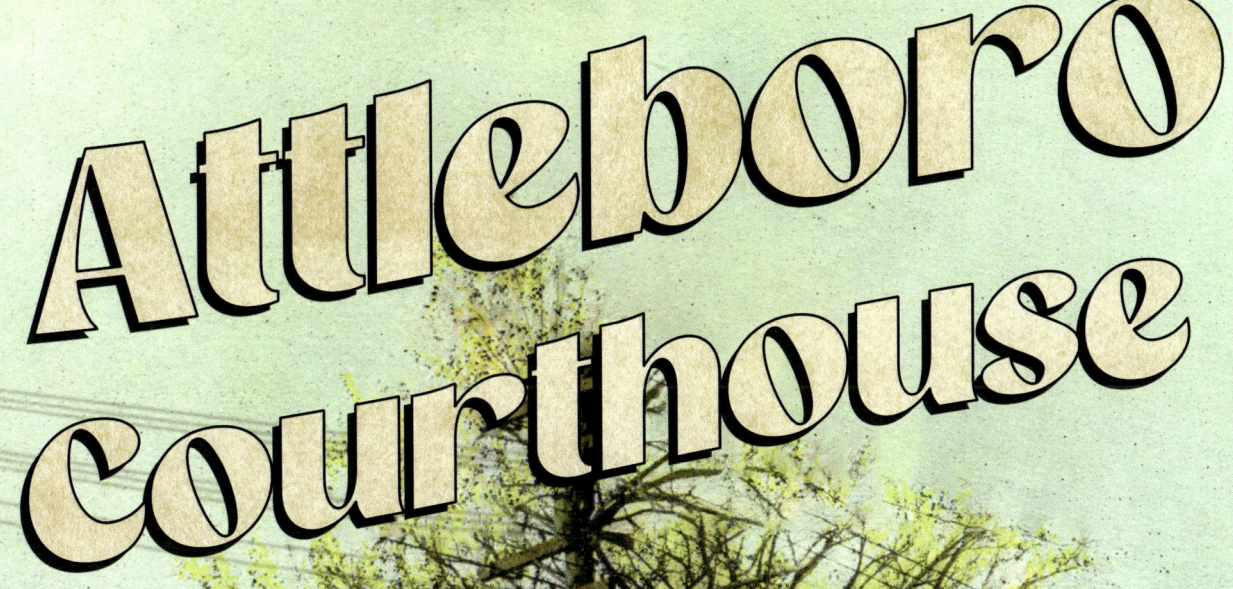

James H. Sullivan Courthouse
Circa 1915 - 1960

James H. Sullivan Courthouse – Attleboro's Neo-Classical Landmark

The James H. Sullivan Courthouse, located at 88 North Main Street in Attleboro, Massachusetts, is a demonstration to early 20th-century civic architecture. Designed by Charles Brigham of the esteemed architectural firm Brigham, Coveney & Bisbee, the courthouse was constructed between 1914 and 1915 in the Neo-Classical style. The building features a red brick and concrete facade, one-story wings on its east and west sides, and a wide white band and cornice accentuating its flat roofline. Originally housing the Fourth District Court, the courthouse served as a cornerstone for justice in the community, handling civil and criminal cases.

Set on landscaped grounds, the courthouse stands as a symbol of Attleboro's growth and modernization during the early 1900s. It boasts three main courtrooms designed to serve the legal needs of a bustling city. The structure's symmetrical design and restrained classical details reflect Brigham's commitment to marrying elegance with practicality, a hallmark of his architectural philosophy.

Over the decades, the courthouse has adapted to modern demands. In 1969, a new wing was added to the northeast side, blending contemporary needs with the historic aesthetic. A devastating electrical fire in 2009 caused significant damage to the civil department offices and two courtrooms. The resulting $900,000 restoration project, completed in 2010 by R.P. Valois & Company, revitalized the 97-year-old building. Upgrades included improved safety measures, compliance with modern codes, and repairs to the masonry and interior spaces, ensuring the building could continue its essential role in the community.

The courthouse remains a focal point of Attleboro's historical and civic life, with its image captured on postcards from the early to mid-20th century. These postcards offer a glimpse into the courthouse's storied past, illustrating its significance as both an architectural and cultural landmark in Attleboro's history.

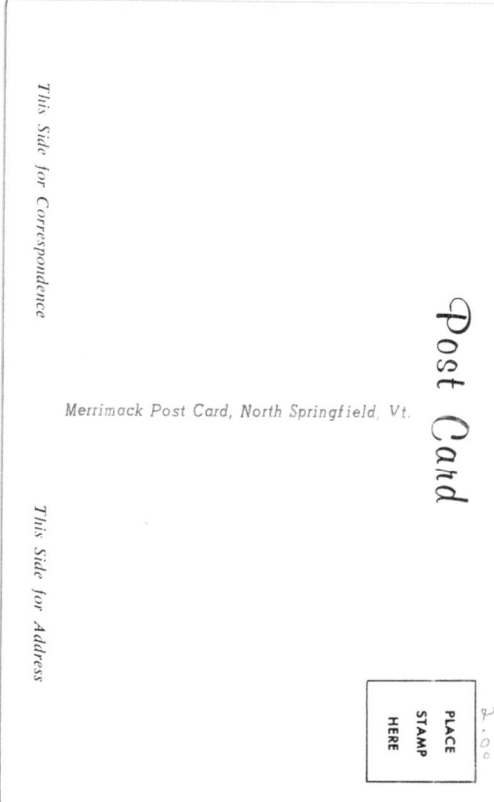

ATTLEBORO COURTHOUSE

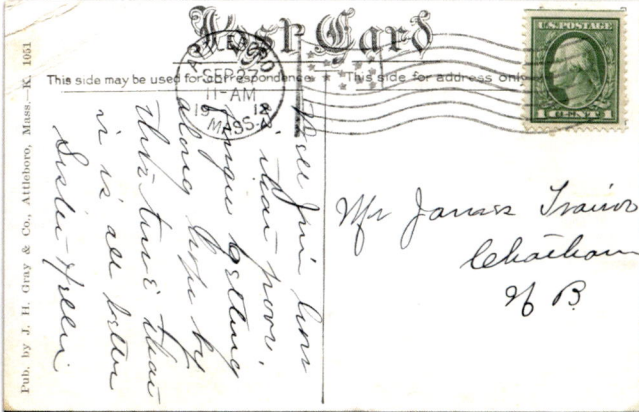

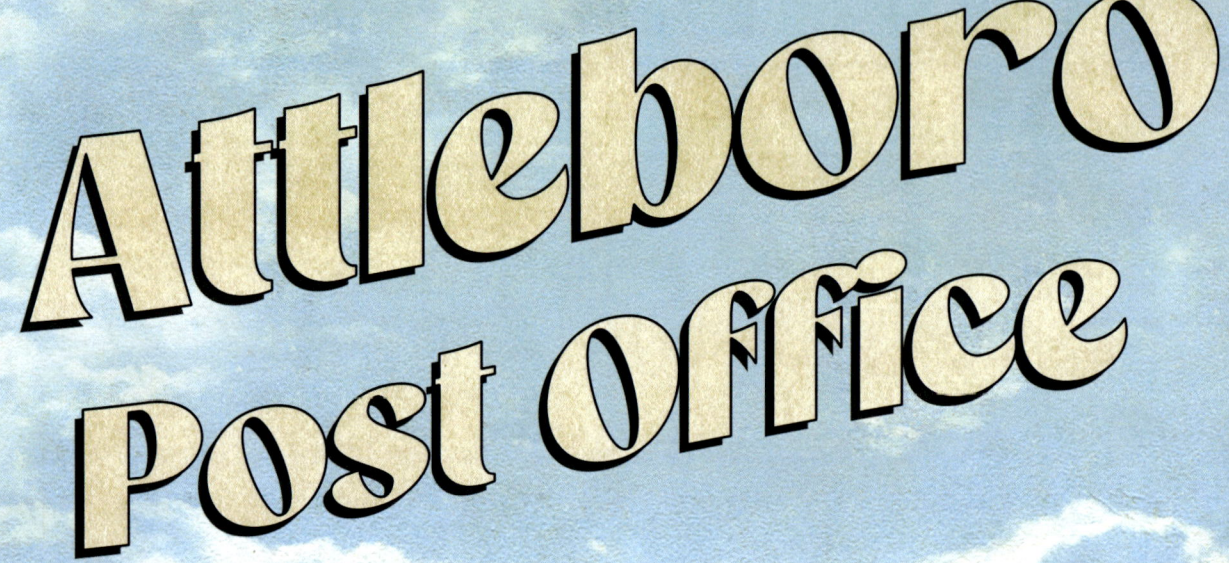

Attleboro Post Office

ATTLEBORO POST OFFICE

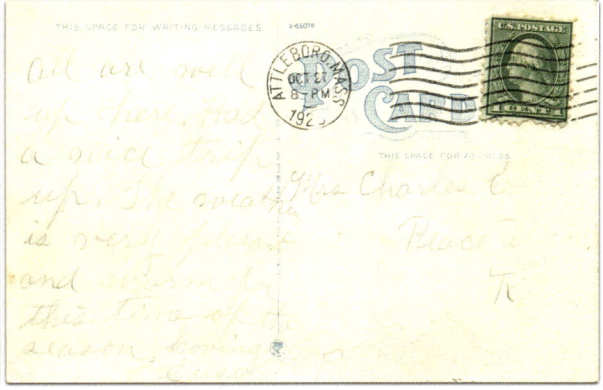

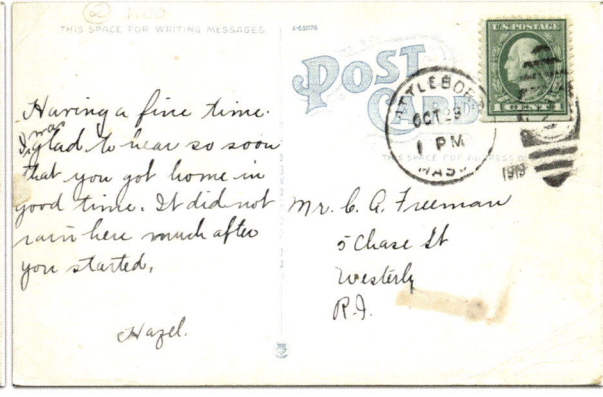

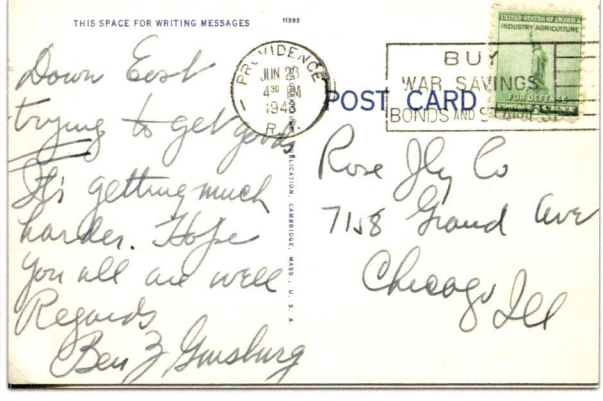

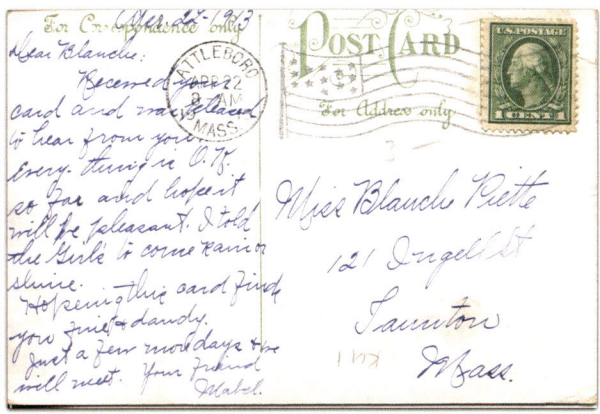

GREETINGS FROM ATTLEBORO

The United States Post Office Building in Attleboro, Massachusetts

The historic United States Post Office Building, located at 75 Park Street in Attleboro, Massachusetts, stands as a testament to the city's architectural heritage and community development. Constructed in 1916 at a cost of $91,000, this Classical Revival structure boasts a commanding presence with its Indiana limestone facade, granite steps, and monumental multi-column design. Inside, the lobby exudes timeless elegance with a patterned marble floor, reflecting the grandeur of early 20th-century civic architecture.

For decades, the building served as Attleboro's primary post office, supporting the town's bustling manufacturing economy and growing population. By the late 19th century, Attleboro had evolved into a hub of industrial activity, known for its jewelry manufacturing. The presence of efficient postal services was vital to the area's economic success, linking local businesses with national and international markets. In addition to the main post office on Park Street, smaller post offices in South Attleboro, Hebronville, Dodgeville, and Brigg's Corner ensured that residents across the region had access to reliable communication services.

In October 1991, the main post office operations were relocated to Pleasant Street, and the historic Park Street building ceased its original function. Three years later, on November 4, 1994, the City of Attleboro purchased the property, repurposing it as a space for local government offices and memorials. Today, it houses a memorial wall dedicated to Towne Crier Larry Fitton, honoring his contributions to the community.

This structure not only reflects Attleboro's rich history but also serves as a tangible reminder of the city's civic pride and its commitment to preserving historical landmarks. As part of the National Register of Historic Places, the Old Attleboro Post Office stands as a cornerstone of the city's heritage, bridging its industrious past with its vibrant present.

Stamps Used In This Postcard Collection
circa 1905 - 1967

ATTLEBORO POST OFFICE

Attleboro Train Station

ATTLEBORO TRAIN STATION

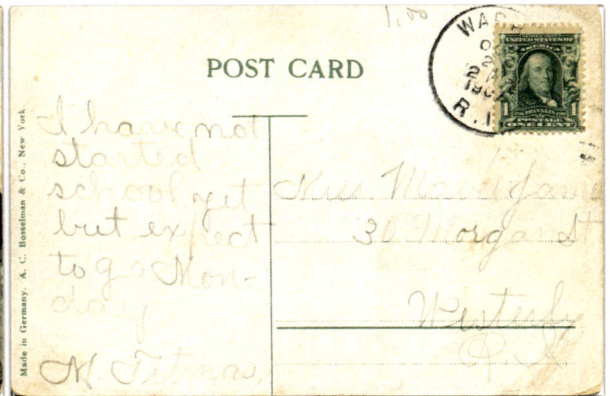

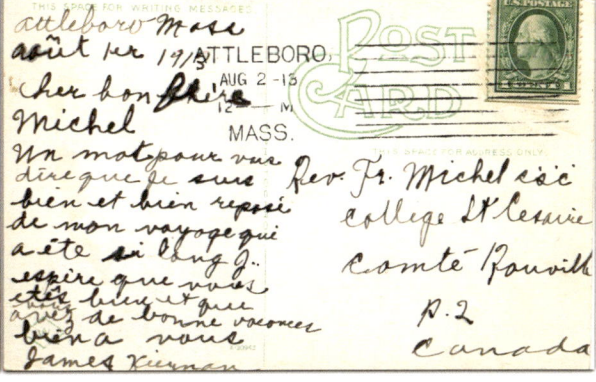

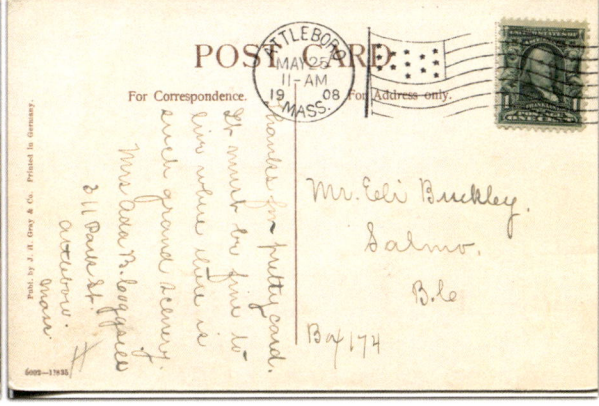

GREETINGS FROM ATTLEBORO

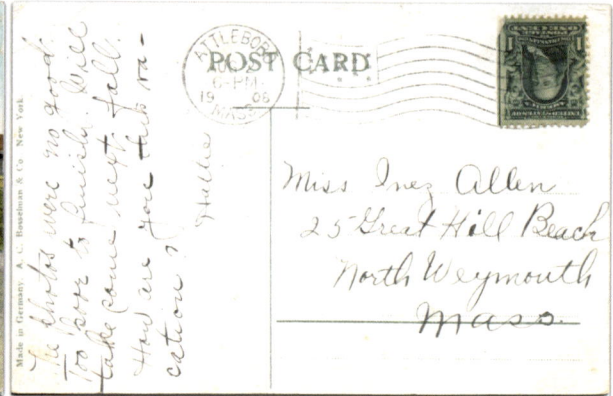

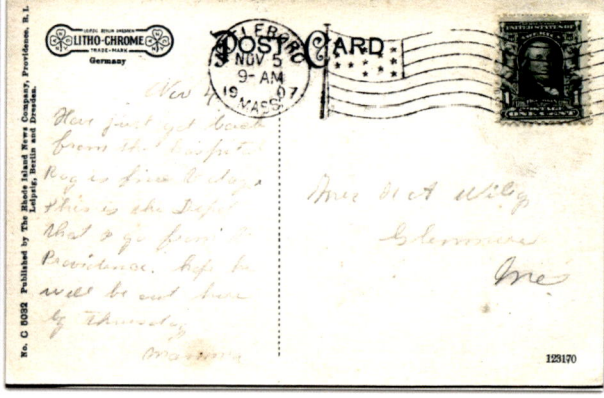

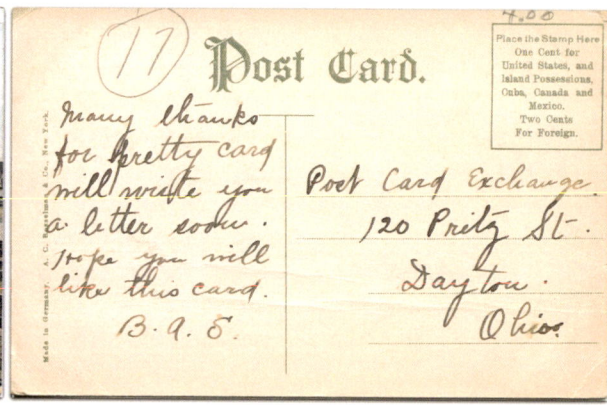

The Attleboro Train Station

The Attleboro Train Station has long been a cornerstone of transportation and community development in Attleboro, Massachusetts. Located at 133 South Main Street, it serves as a vital link between Boston's South Station and southern destinations like Providence, Rhode Island. The station offers convenience for commuters and travelers alike, beyond its modern-day functionality, the station holds a rich history that reflects the growth and evolution of Attleboro as a vibrant community.

Railroad service in Attleboro dates back to 1835, marking the beginning of its significance as a transportation hub. By the early 1900s, when postcards depicting the station were widely circulated, the train station was at the height of its importance. It facilitated the movement of goods, people, and ideas, playing a crucial role in the city's industrial boom. During this period, Attleboro was emerging as a prominent center for jewelry manufacturing. The train station enabled the swift transportation of raw materials and finished goods, linking local artisans with broader markets across the region and beyond. This connectivity fueled economic growth and helped establish Attleboro as the "Jewelry Capital of the World."

The station's design reflects the architectural style of the era, with two-story northbound and southbound buildings that now house private businesses. These structures were bustling hubs of activity in the early 20th century, where passengers awaited trains, shipments were loaded and unloaded, and the community gathered. The station's central location in downtown Attleboro made it a focal point of daily life, contributing to the city's growth as a center of commerce and culture.

A transformative development in the early 20th century was the installation of grade crossing bridges. These bridges were critical in improving safety and efficiency as they eliminated the need for trains and pedestrians to navigate at-grade crossings. The innovative infrastructure reduced the risk of accidents and allowed trains to run more smoothly and reliably. This advancement not only enhanced the station's functionality but also underscored its importance as a safe and modern transportation link.

Today, the Attleboro Train Station continues to connect people to opportunities and experiences, serving as both a practical transit hub and a reminder of the city's rich history. From its roots in the early days of rail travel to its ongoing contributions to regional connectivity, the station remains a symbol of progress, resilience, and community pride. As a gateway to arts, culture, and historic landmarks along the Providence/Stoughton Line, the station's legacy endures as an integral part of Attleboro's story.

GREETINGS FROM ATTLEBORO

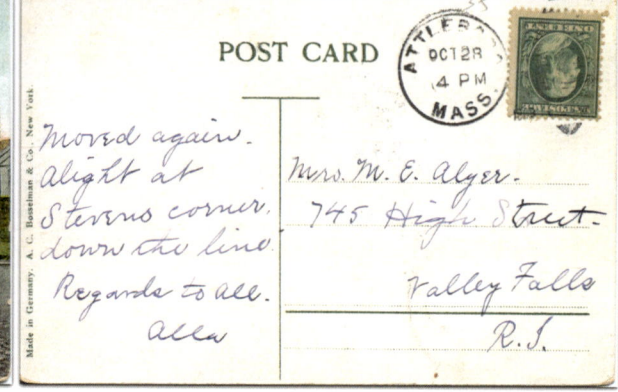

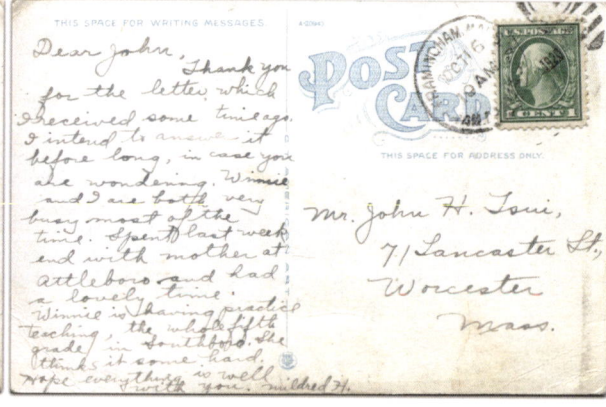

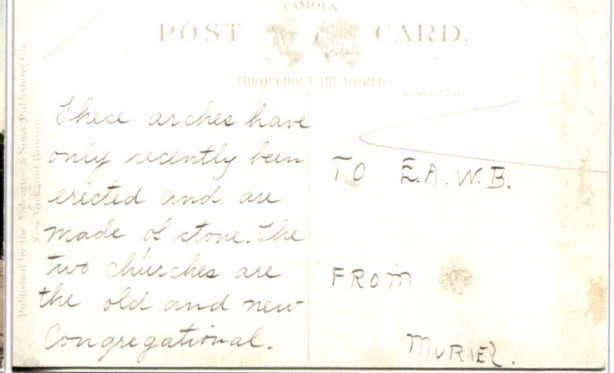

ATTLEBORO TRAIN STATION

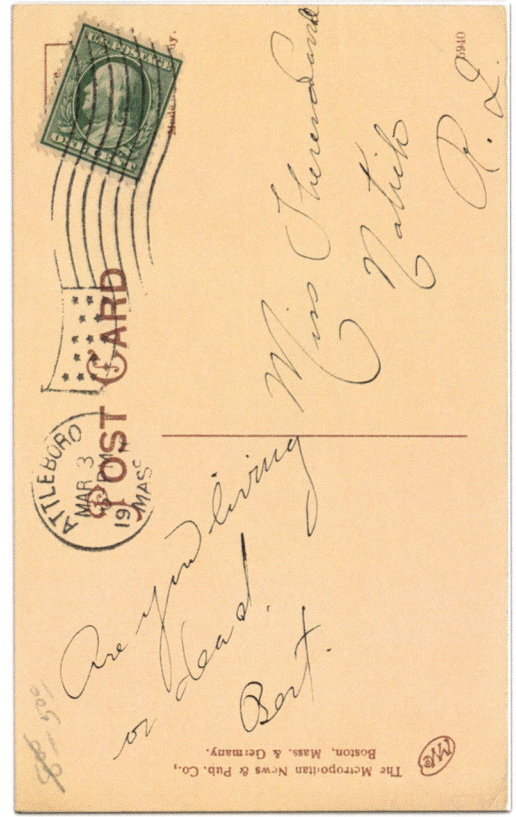

Postal Mysteries: Live or Dead?

The postmark on this intriguing postcard dates back to March 3, 1910—a small yet captivating slice of history from over a century ago. Sent from Bert to Miss Sherenda in Natick, Rhode Island, the message is as peculiar as it is succinct: **"Are you living or dead?"**

At first glance, this cryptic note raises more questions than answers. Was it a joke, an inside quip between friends, or something more profound? In the context of the era, communication often carried both charm and mystery, especially in an age when postcards were a favorite medium for quick correspondence.

The postcard, depicting the Attleboro Train Station, likely traveled along the bustling railways of New England, perhaps passing through the historic Attleboro Station. Established as part of the Boston and Providence Railroad, the station was a vital hub, connecting communities across Massachusetts and Rhode Island. By 1910, the station had been modernized, reflecting the growing importance of rail travel and the vibrancy of the region. The journey of this postcard mirrors the energy of early 20th-century life: swift, direct, and layered with untold stories.

Beyond the message, the postcard serves as a quiet reminder to the daily exchanges that knit communities together. Whether Bert's words were penned with humor or genuine curiosity, they highlight the unique and often playful nature of personal correspondence from a bygone era.

Today, we are left to wonder about the relationship between Bert and Miss Sherenda—*much like Schrödinger's thought experiment; I wonder if Miss Sherenda has a cat?* This tiny piece of history continues to spark imagination, serving as both a bridge between the past and the present and a reminder that sometimes, life's greatest mysteries come with a wink and a question mark.

Schrödinger's Cat: Unlocking the Mystery of Quantum Superposition

Schrödinger's Cat is a thought experiment illustrating quantum superposition—a key concept in quantum mechanics. Imagine a cat inside a sealed box containing radioactive material, a Geiger counter, poison, and a hammer. If the radioactive atom decays, the Geiger counter triggers the hammer to release poison, killing the cat. Quantum theory suggests the atom is simultaneously decayed and undecayed until observed. Thus, before opening, the cat is theoretically both alive and dead simultaneously. This paradox emphasizes quantum uncertainty and questions how or if superposition applies to larger, everyday objects, challenging our intuitive understanding of reality ... or perhaps Miss Sherenda's status.

GREETINGS FROM ATTLEBORO

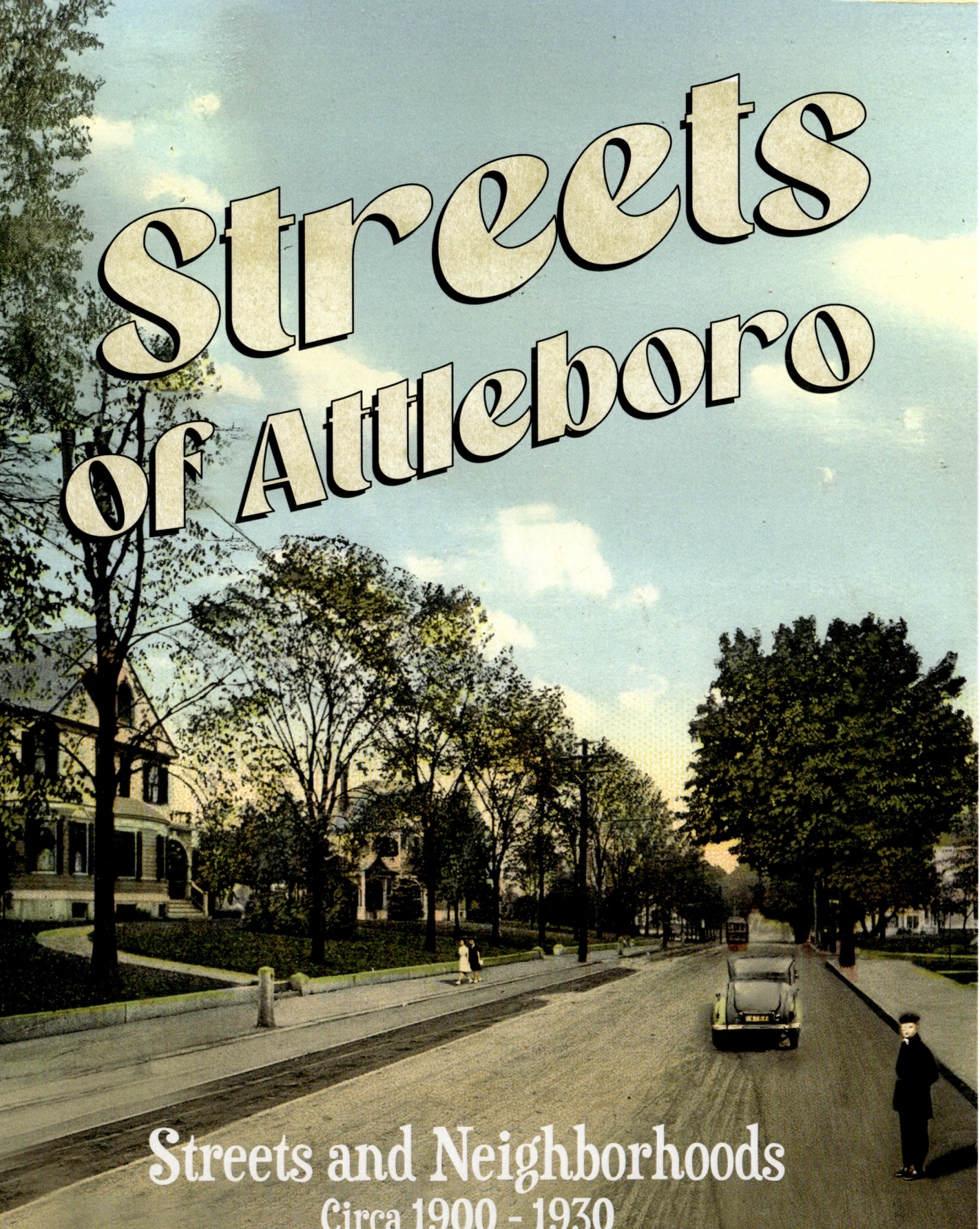

GREETINGS FROM ATTLEBORO

A Walk Through Attleboro's Streets: A Glimpse of the Past Through Postcards

Attleboro's streets hold stories woven through time, a demonstration to the town's evolution from its quiet origins to its bustling present. Through the postcards collected over the years, we gain a picturesque look at the neighborhoods of early 20th-century Attleboro. These visual relics invite us to glimpse the daily lives of the town's residents, framed by tree-lined paths and tranquil surroundings.

With just a handful of postcards, the differences between then and now become strikingly clear. Yet, with a bit of imagination and a discerning eye, familiar details emerge—a building that still stands, a street layout that endures. These streets speak of a town that grew steadily, shaped by industry and human connection. Much like veins in a body, they carried the lifeblood of trade, intersecting railways and rivers while also serving as the stage for social interactions; residents walking hand-in-hand, children riding bikes, and in later years, electric railcars gliding alongside early automobiles. These images reflect a town not just surviving but thriving, its streets alive with purpose and community.

The postcards themselves are more than simple images; they are miniature works of art, imbued with both technological advancement and personal sentiment. Produced during a period of rapid innovation in photography and printing, they serve as relics of a bygone era. Hand-tinted colors and meticulous photographic techniques make each postcard unique, capturing moments in time with a vibrancy that transcends the medium.

These cards were not merely souvenirs but mementos, meant to be shared and cherished. The handwritten notes on their backs often added another layer of significance. A quick scrawl—***"Made it home safe"***—or a thoughtful message referencing a specific street corner transformed these postcards into personal connections between sender and recipient. The tactile nature of holding a postcard, knowing that it was penned by another's hand with intention, creates a sense of intimacy often missing in today's digital communications. Through these cards, we can feel the rhythm of life in Attleboro during an era when such exchanges were commonplace yet deeply meaningful.

The everyday life reflected in these postcards paints a picture of simplicity and warmth. A postcard from Grace in 1910 captures this spirit: ***"If you look far enough up this street, you'll see us in the front window writing this card..."*** In these few words, Grace encapsulates the small-town charm and personal connections that defined Attleboro's streets. Messages like Grace's reveal a practical yet sentimental use of postcards. Often used for quick updates or lighthearted musings, they reflected the straightforward communication of the time. The cards themselves became windows to the world for their recipients, offering a glimpse into Attleboro's quiet beauty and bustling energy. They provide modern readers with invaluable insights into how residents lived, worked, and connected.

Transformation Over Time

Though the streets depicted in these postcards still exist today, they would be nearly unrecognizable to someone from a century ago. As automobiles became commonplace in the 1920s, the demand for wider, better-regulated streets grew. Attleboro, a town bustling with manufacturers and commerce, saw its streets transition into crucial arteries of trade. Roads extended outward, connecting the town to the larger region and beyond, while providing residents with greater mobility and opportunity.

By the 1950s and 1960s, the tree-lined sidewalks that once shaded pedestrians gave way to the increasing need for road expansions. Entire sections of greenery were sacrificed to accommodate the growing number of cars. In some cases, streets were widened by as much as 15 feet, reshaping the landscape around downtown Attleboro. While these changes brought progress and accessibility, they also marked the end of a quieter, slower-paced era.

At their core, streets are more than mere pathways. They connect homes, businesses, and people, serving as the framework upon which communities are built. In Attleboro, these streets have carried the weight of commerce and the laughter of children, the bustle of parades, and the quiet steps of a neighbor's stroll. The postcards remind us that streets are not static; they are dynamic spaces where history and human stories intersect.

Today, as we walk or drive these same streets, we tread upon the echoes of the past. The postcards offer a reminder that even as the landscape changes, the essence of connection remains. Through them, we see how streets have not only shaped the physical structure of Attleboro but also its identity, making them more than just roads—they are the lifeblood of a community.

GREETINGS FROM ATTLEBORO

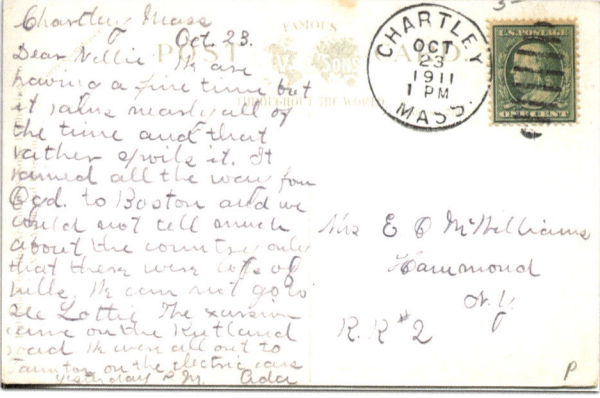

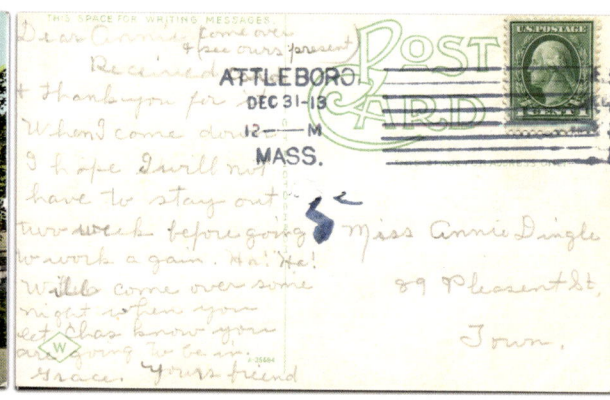

STREETS AND NEIGHBORHOODS

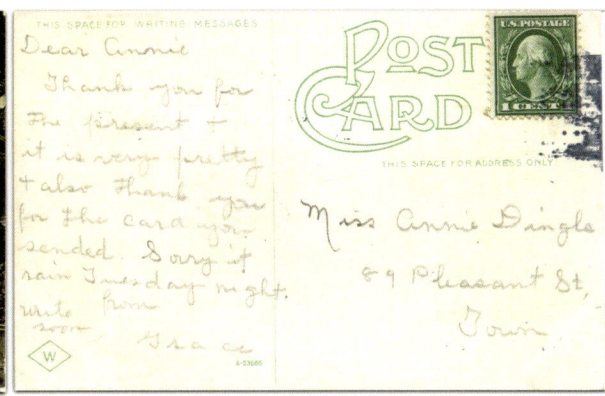

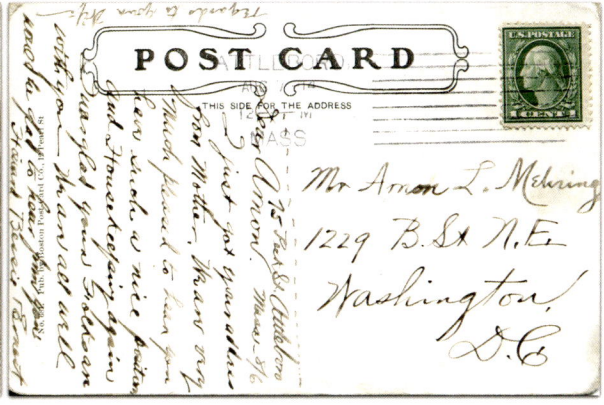

GREETINGS FROM ATTLEBORO

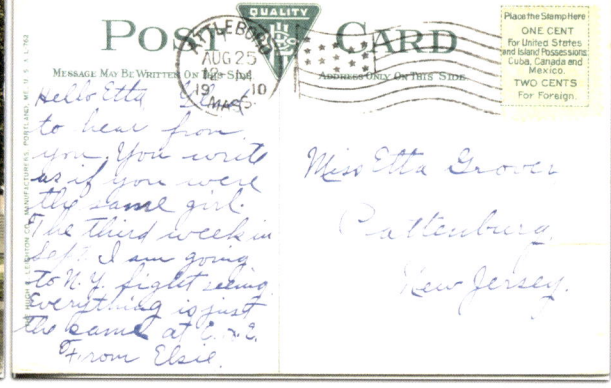

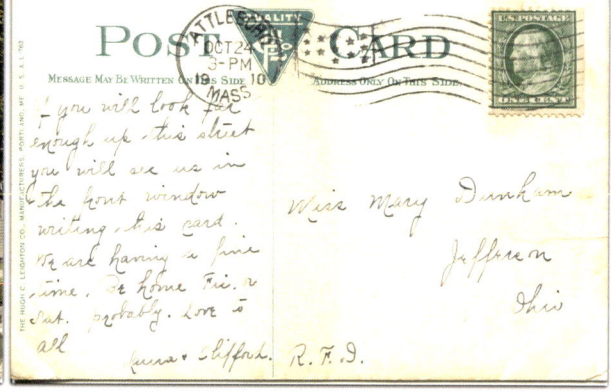

STREETS AND NEIGHBORHOODS

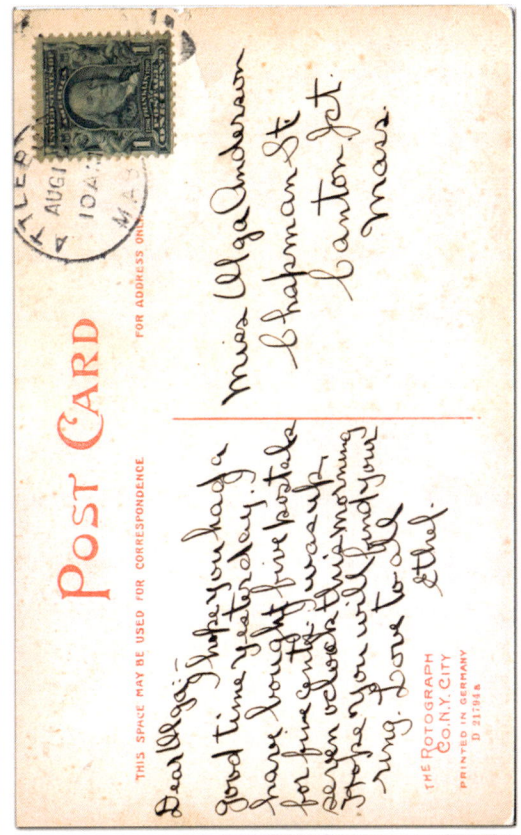

A Penny (or two) for Your Thoughts

In 1908, a single cent stamp was all it took to send a postcard across the country. This seemingly insignificant amount bridged distances and allowed people to share snippets of their lives. In Ethel's words, captured on one such postcard: "I have bought five postcards for five cents.", accompany this with a 1-cent Benjamin Franklin stamp, and the postcard has become a symbol of the era's efficiency and simplicity.

Postcards at this time were more than just a means of communication—they were a cultural phenomenon. A booming industry emerged, with designs showcasing picturesque landscapes, bustling cities, and charming local landmarks. This affordability, combined with their visual appeal, made postcards accessible to nearly everyone.

By contrast, today's postcards and stamps tell a very different story. A single postcard in 2025 averages $1 to $5, depending on its design and size, and postcard stamps still offer a discount over letter stamps, with; at the time of writing, the cost of 56 cents compared to the 73 cents of a standard stamp. Adjusted for inflation, a 1908 penny is equivalent to about 30 cents today, meaning postcards have become significantly more expensive. What was once an everyday luxury now feels like a quaint novelty.

The rise in cost reflects changes in materials, production, and postal infrastructure over the decades. Additionally, while postcards were once a primary mode of communication, they now compete with instant messaging and digital platforms. The decline in demand has influenced their pricing, making them more of a collectible or artistic expression than a necessity. Despite these changes, postcards retain a nostalgic charm. They continue to connect us with history, echoing simpler times when a penny and a thoughtful message were all you needed to stay in touch.

Benjamin Franklin 1-cent Stamp

The United States Postal Office issued the Benjamin Franklin 1-cent Scotts 316 on February 18th, 1908. The stamp was printed using the flat plate printing method. Scotts 316 is blue-green, and it has a double-lined watermark. The 1908 1¢ Franklin coil stamp (#316) was issued experimentally by the USPS in horizontal coil format, primarily for vending machine use. Printed via flat plate, this stamp featured a design inspired by Joseph-Siffred Duplessis's 1778 Franklin portrait. Coil stamps emerged alongside vending machines to offer convenient access to postage stamps, reflecting an era of postal innovation.

A Night at the Movies

The postcard, dated October 27, 1933, offers a heartfelt glimpse into the life of "Cal," who penned a hurried message to Mr. and Mrs. W. T. Libbey in Gray, Maine. While the front of the card depicts North Main Street in Attleboro, the back carries the excited scrawl of someone eager to prepare for an evening out. Cal's words, *"I am in a hurry to get dressed and go to the movies tonight,"* capture the anticipation of attending a film at the Union Theater, a jewel of Attleboro that had opened just five years earlier in 1928.

By 1933, the Union Theater had become a centerpiece of entertainment in the city, offering a glamorous escape from the challenges of the Great Depression. Moviegoers flocked to its grand marquee to enjoy the latest Hollywood hits. Based on the postcard's postmark, Cal might have been preparing to watch one of several notable films from that October lineup. **I'm No Angel**, released October 6, starred the inimitable Mae West in one of her most iconic roles. **Riders of Destiny,** an early John Wayne film, hit the screens on October 10, delighting fans of Westerns. And by October 21, **Footlight Parade** brought spectacular Busby Berkeley choreography to the big screen.

For Cal, attending a movie in 1933 wasn't just about the film—it was an experience of community and wonder. The Union Theater, with its plush seating, ornate decor, and lively crowds, offered a much-needed escape and a touch of magic in an otherwise challenging time. This postcard's human aspect reminds us of the thrill of these outings, where films were a shared cultural event, a reason to dress up, and an opportunity to be transported to another world.

The joy captured in Cal's words serves as a timeless reminder of how cinema has shaped our lives, bringing us together to laugh, dream, and marvel at stories larger than life.

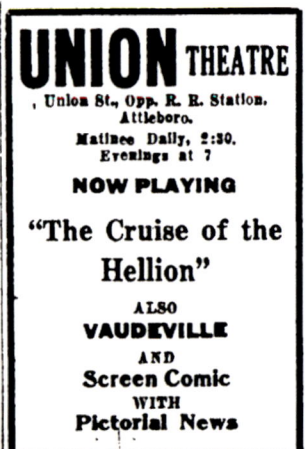

*Advertisement for Union Theatre
April 27, 1928. Pawtucket Times.
image credit: cinematreasures.org*

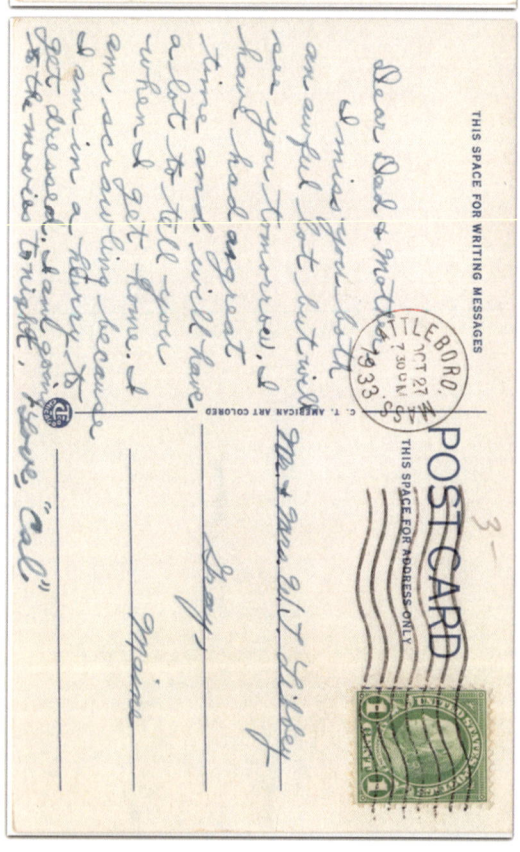

"The Numbers - Movies Released in 1933." The Numbers, Nash Information Services,
www.the-numbers.com/movies/year/1933. Accessed 28 Jan. 2025.

STREETS AND NEIGHBORHOODS

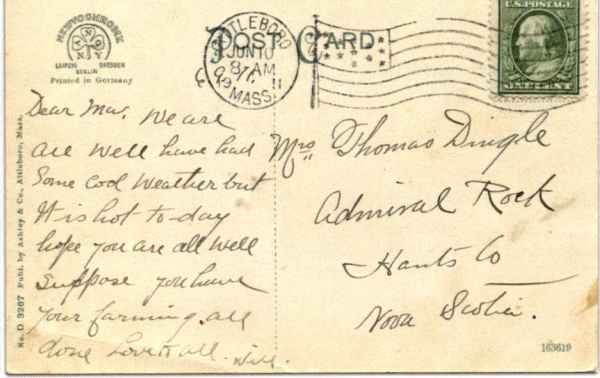

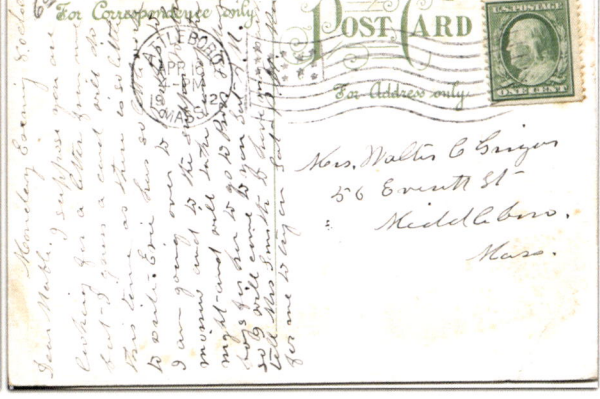

GREETINGS FROM ATTLEBORO

COUNTY STREET, LOOKING WEST, OPPOSITE CAPRON PARK, ATTLEBORO, MASS.

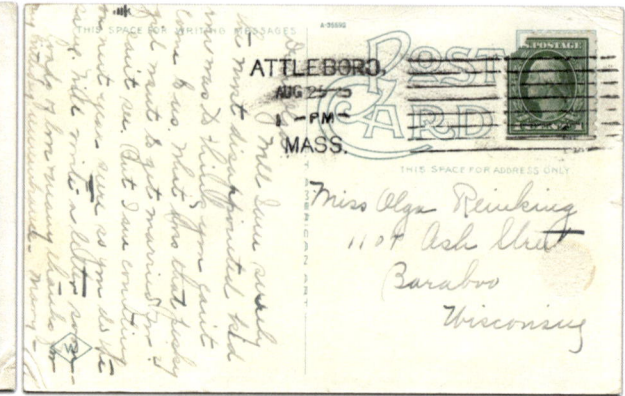

County Street looking Northeast, Attleboro, Mass.

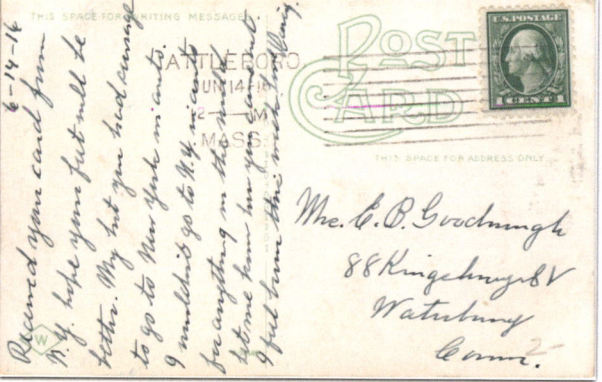

On County Street, Attleboro, Mass.

COUNTY STREET, LOOKING WEST, OPPOSITE CAPRON PARK, ATTLEBORO, MASS.

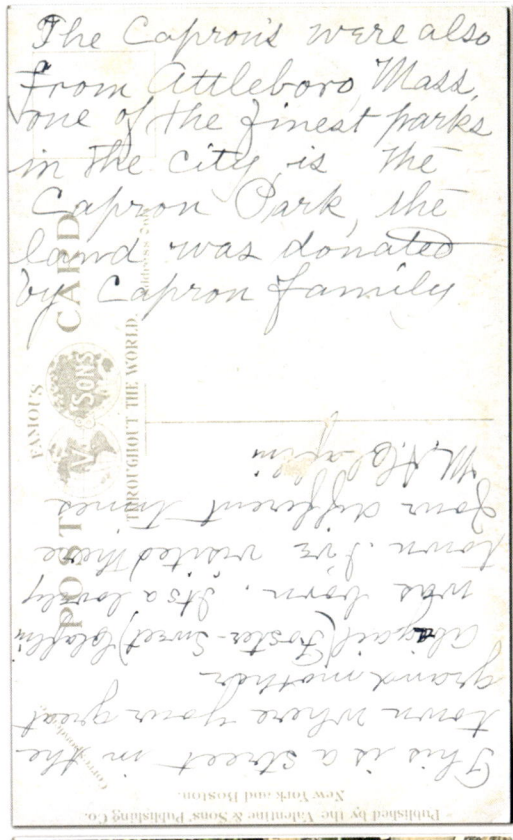

The Capron Family: From Stowaway to Attleboro Legacy

In 1674, 14-year-old Banfield Capron embarked on a life-changing journey across the Atlantic Ocean, stowing away with three friends aboard a ship bound for the New World. Discovered after four days at sea, the captain initially planned to return them to England, but passengers persuaded him otherwise. The reasons for Banfield's daring escape remain unknown—whether fleeing hardship or seeking adventure—but his arrival in Attleboro, then known as the "North Purchase," marked the beginning of a remarkable legacy.

Banfield Capron quickly established himself as industrious and successful, acquiring significant landholdings. He married three times and fathered 12 children, including Joseph Capron, born in 1691. The Caprons' contributions extended far beyond land and legacy. Seth Capron, Banfield's great-great-grandson, served as a doctor and soldier in the Revolutionary War at just 19. Legend has it that Seth narrowly survived a cannonball intended for General Marquis de Lafayette and later commanded a barge carrying George Washington as he bid farewell to his officers.

The Capron family's prominence continued through Horace Capron Jr., who earned the Congressional Medal of Honor for valor at the Battle of Gaines' Mill during the Civil War. Items from their storied history—including medals, swords, and binoculars used by Union General Horace Capron Sr.—are preserved at the Park and Forestry Department headquarters in Attleboro.

Today, Residences such as Marian Wrightington continue to perserve the very hosue *(pictured below)* that the Caprons once resided in dating back to 1740. Additional landmarks such as Capron Park, donated to the city in 1901 by Dennis Capron's children, and later, Capron Park Zoo opened in 1937 on 8 acres of the donated land, stand as enduring symbols of the family's contributions to Attleboro's history and community and has become one of the most pronounced families in Attleboro. Not bad for a Stowaway teenager from a faraway land.

Capron, Circa 1910 - 1940

Wrightington, Circa 1967

GREETINGS FROM ATTLEBORO

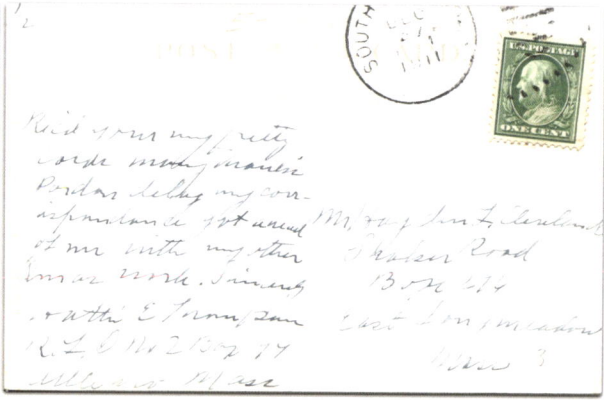

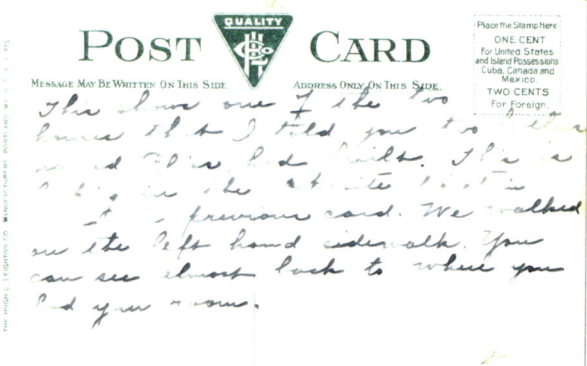

STREETS AND NEIGHBORHOODS

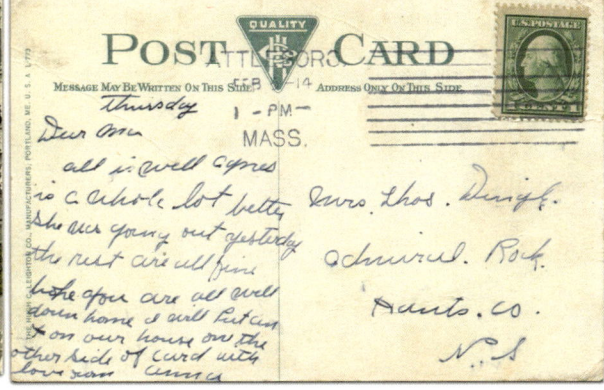

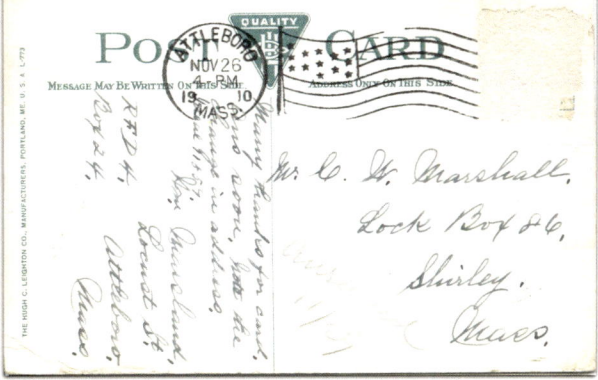

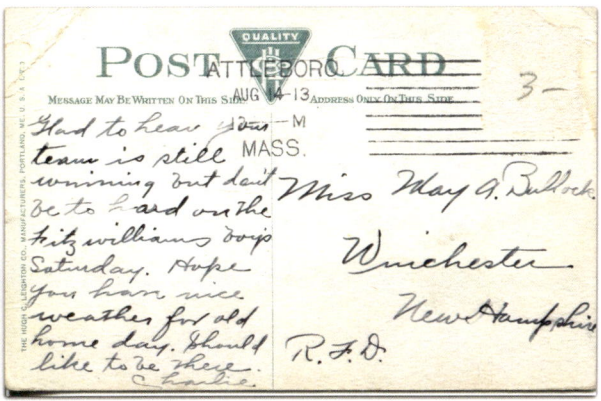

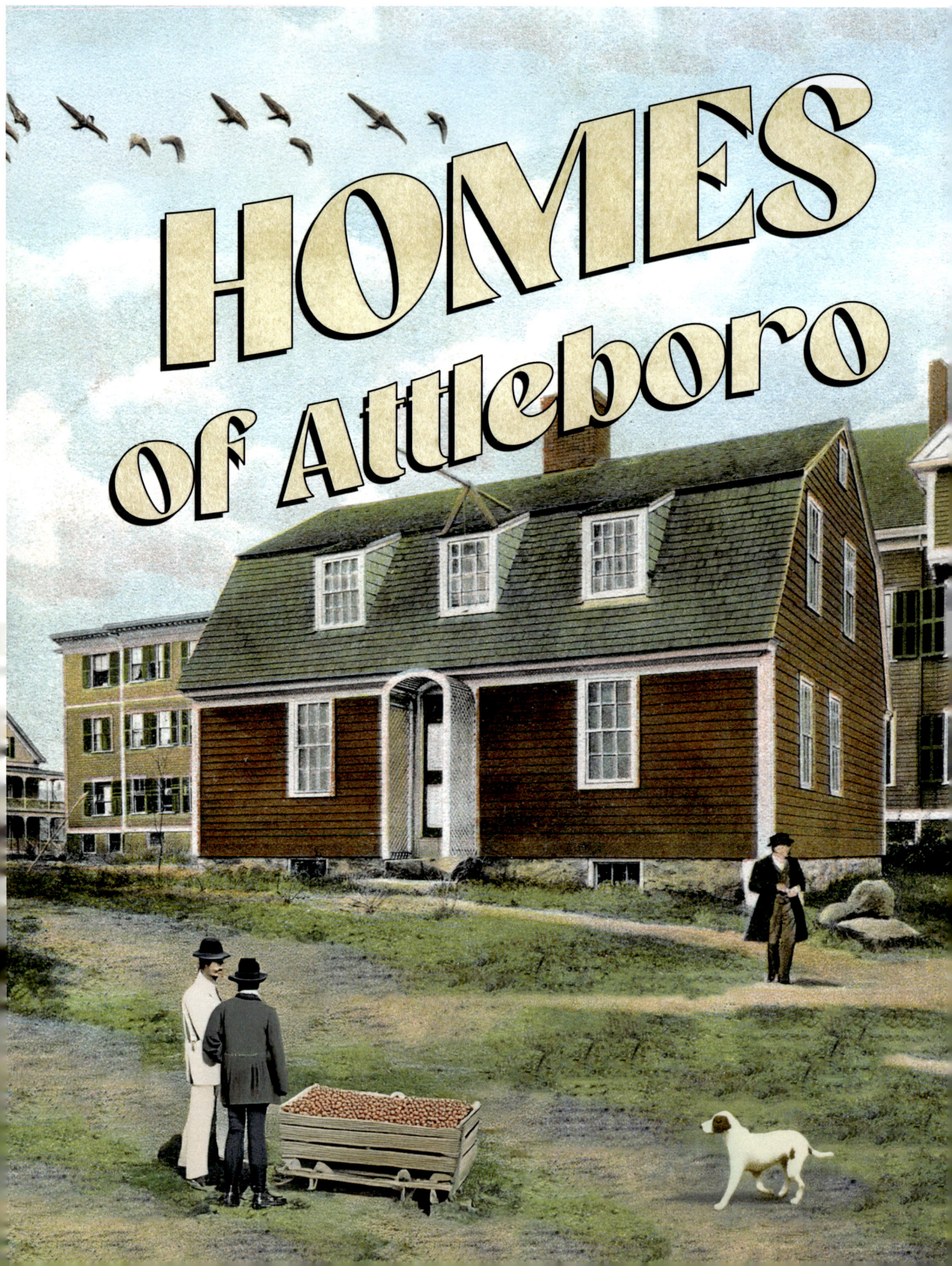

HOMES OF ATTLEBORO

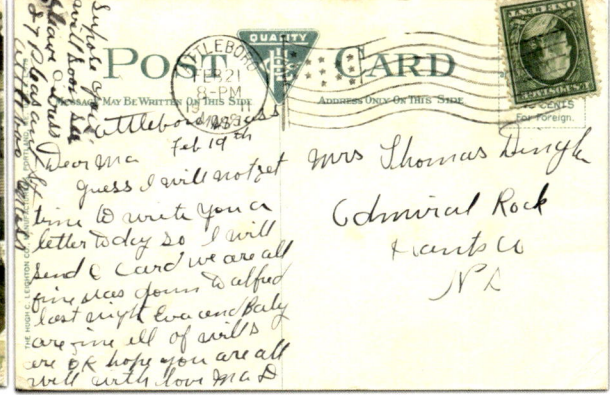

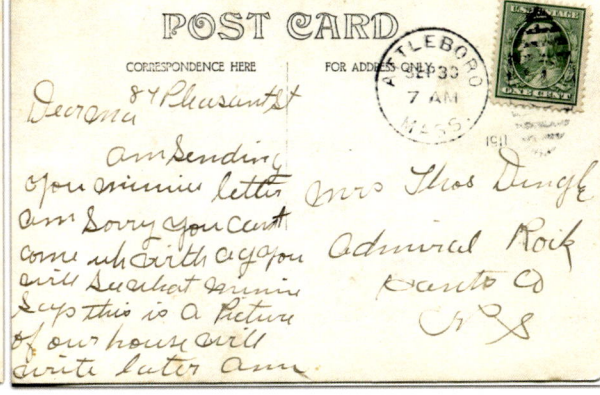

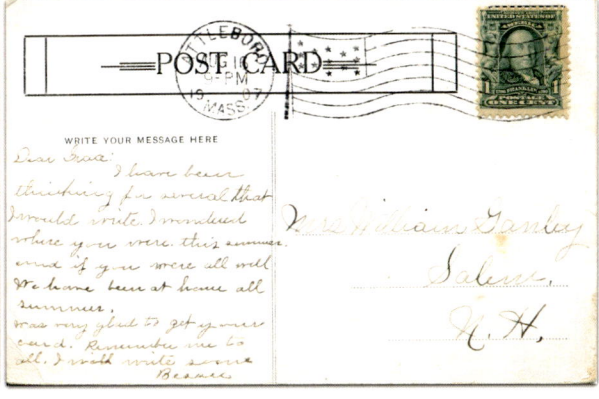

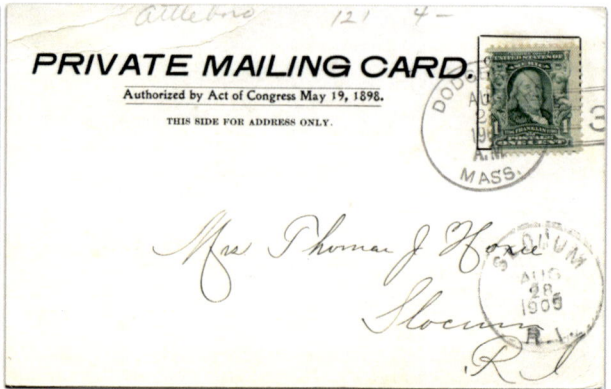

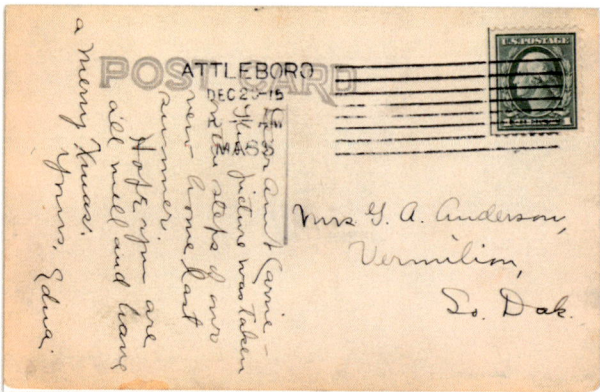

The Historic Homes of Attleboro

The postcards in this collection capture the essence of Attleboro's rich architectural and historical legacy, with several homes holding deep significance to the town's heritage. Many of these residences were celebrated during Attleboro's Old Home Week, an event dedicated to honoring the town's past and its longstanding families.

Among the notable homes is the Old Holman Homestead, a well-preserved example of colonial architecture, featuring a picturesque winter scene on one postcard. This home was a gathering place for generations and reflects the enduring charm of 18th and 19th-century New England homesteads. Another significant property is the Old Peck House, once owned by the Daughters of the American Revolution, highlighting its historical importance in preserving local Revolutionary-era heritage.

Other postcards feature rustic, centuries-old homesteads with classic New England elements such as stone walls, wooden clapboards, and hand-pumped wells, showcasing the self-sufficient rural lifestyles of Attleboro's early settlers. The Woodacre Tourist Home and Cottages adds a glimpse of Attleboro's role in early 20th-century travel, demonstrating how the town catered to visitors before the rise of modern motels.

Each of these homes, whether standing today or lost to time, tells a unique story of Attleboro's evolution from a colonial settlement to a thriving industrial town. Through these postcards, we gain not just visual history but a deeper connection to the families, traditions, and events that shaped the community.

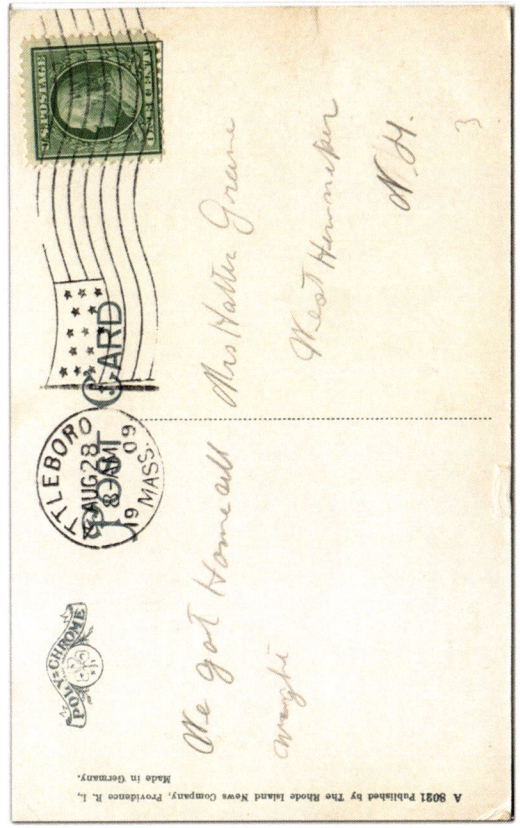

Attleboro's Hospital and Care

The Legacy of Sturdy Memorial Hospital in Attleboro

Sturdy Memorial Hospital, a cornerstone of healthcare in Attleboro, traces its roots to a generous act of philanthropy. Ellen A. Winsor, daughter of James and Adah Sturdy, bequeathed her family's Victorian mansion and estate to the town with the intent of establishing a hospital. Recognizing the financial burden such an endeavor would place on local taxpayers, a not-for-profit corporation was formed under Massachusetts law, ensuring the hospital's creation and long-term sustainability.

On April 14, 1913, Sturdy Memorial Hospital officially opened in the former Sturdy mansion, initially operating as a modest 15-bed facility. Over the decades, it expanded to meet the growing needs of the region, bolstered by the dedication of physicians, nurses, volunteers, and community donors. Through their efforts, Sturdy evolved from a small community hospital into a comprehensive healthcare system, now known as Sturdy Health, encompassing a 128-bed acute care hospital and 26 specialty and primary care practices across Southeast Massachusetts and Rhode Island.

For over 110 years, Sturdy has remained steadfast in its commitment to compassionate care and medical excellence. Today, it continues to build on its legacy with modern advancements, including facility expansions and improved patient services. Rooted in the vision of its benefactors, Sturdy Memorial Hospital stands as a beacon to community-driven healthcare, ensuring generations to come receive the care they need.

Sturdy Health. "Our History." Sturdy Memorial Hospital, Sturdy Health, https://www.sturdyhealth.org/about-us/history/. Accessed 4 Feb. 2025.

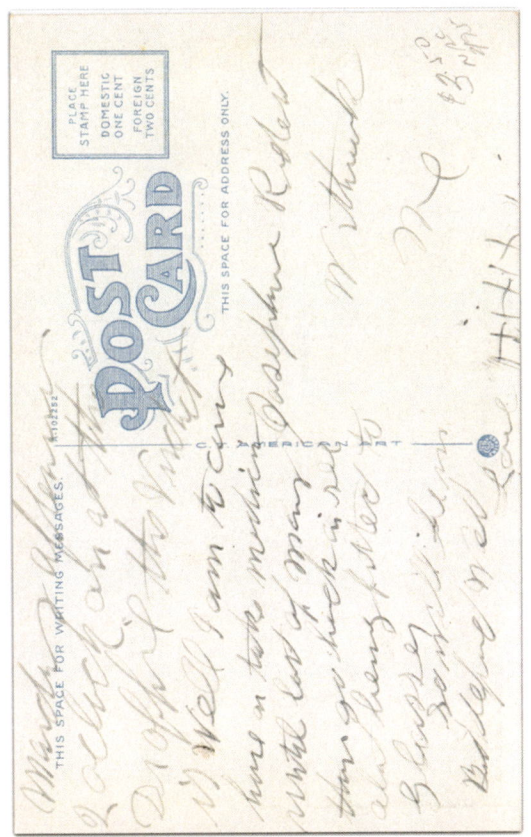

GREETINGS FROM ATTLEBORO

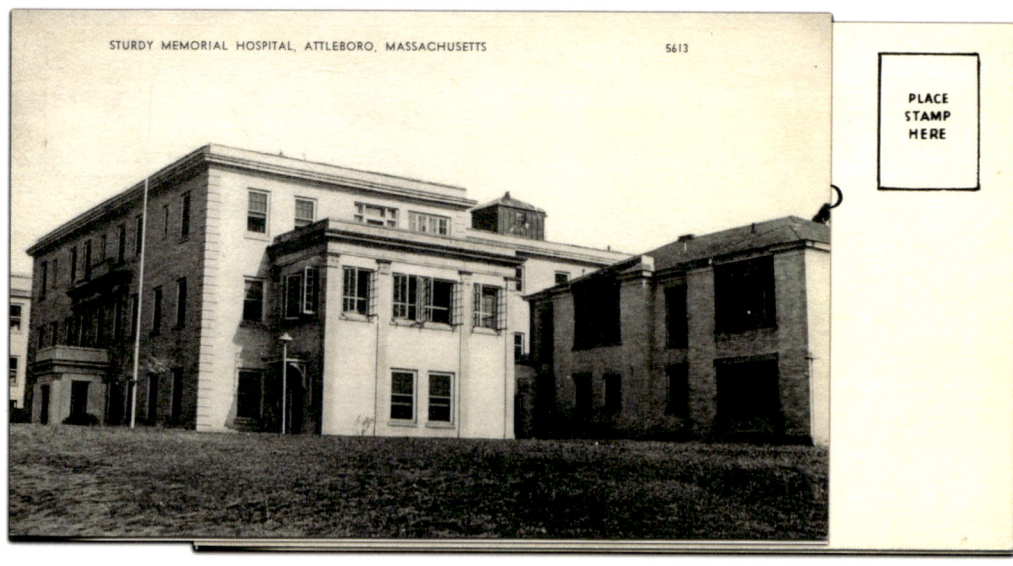

GREETINGS FROM ATTLEBORO

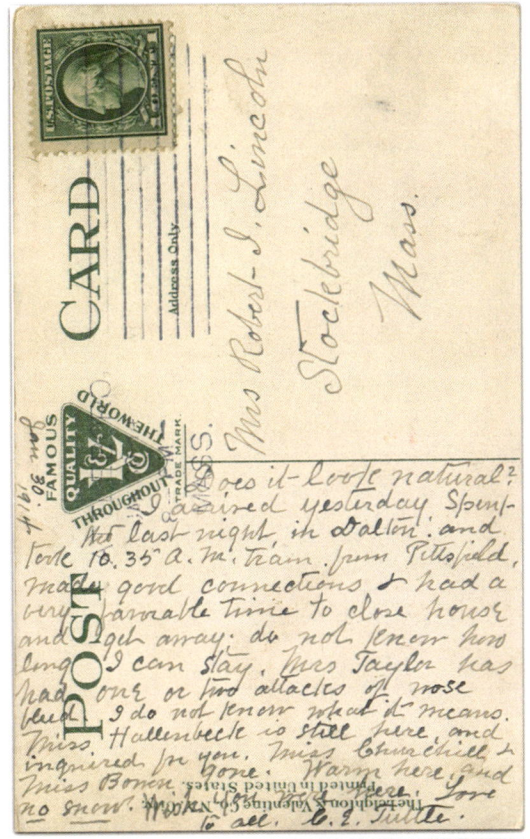

Solomon's Sanatorium: A Grand Dream and a Tragic End

In the late 19th century, a man named James M. Solomon walked the wooded lands of Attleboro, Massachusetts, collecting herbs and roots for his self-made remedies. Although he was widely known as "Dr. Solomon," he was not a licensed medical doctor. Instead, he was a self-styled healer with a grand vision—an expansive sanatorium where people suffering from cancer could find healing.

With determination and ambition, Solomon set his sights on bringing his dream to life. In 1894, he commissioned a civil engineer to survey the land, and by 1901, the sanatorium's walls stood, awaiting their massive roof. However, the project nearly faltered due to a lack of funds—until a local businessman, John M. Fisher, stepped in to provide the necessary financial backing. The final cost of the grand facility reached an astonishing $400,000—a small fortune at the time.

The long-anticipated dedication of Solomon's Sanatorium took place on April 25, 1903. The day was marked by a festive band concert on the Attleboro Common, followed by a parade through the town leading up to the facility itself. The program boasted impressive construction statistics: 475,709 bricks, 309 windows, 3,254 panes of glass, 21 fireplaces, 200 rooms, and an astounding 27 miles of electrical wiring.

A witness to the opening night described the spectacle in glowing terms:

"With the coming of the dark, Dr. Solomon's dream sprang to life in a great blaze of electrical splendor; 1,800 electric lights outlined the exterior of the building, while an immense searchlight mounted on the roof threw its slender, graceful finger of light over four miles."

For a time, the sanatorium thrived. However, financial troubles forced its closure in 1906. The facility reopened in 1908 under the management of the Nicola family, a group of doctors from Battle Creek, Michigan. It operated successfully for a decade before closing again in 1918.

In 1919, the Methodist Church purchased the property, renaming it Attleboro Springs Sanatorium, a nod to the natural springs on the grounds. Though it continued to serve the community, it struggled financially and ultimately shut down in 1938.

In 1942, the La Salette missionaries acquired the property, transforming it into a major seminary. The landmark structure stood until November 5, 1999, when a devastating fire consumed the historic building, tragically killing a visiting English priest. The once-grand sanatorium was torn down, fading into history—forgotten by many but remembered by those who still speak of Solomon's dream and the light that once shone from its rooftop.

Author (if known). "Attleboro Springs Sanitarium Remnants." ADE07 Blog, 7 Mar. 2007, https://ade07.blogspot.com/2007/03/attleboro-springs-sanitarium-remnants.html. Accessed 4 Feb. 2025.
"Attleboro Sanitarium." Asylum Projects, www.asylumprojects.org/index.php/Attleboro_Sanitarium. Accessed 4 Feb. 2025.

A Narrow Escape: The Fisher Automobile Accident of the Early 1900s

In the early 1900s, the streets of Attleboro bore witness to both the marvel and menace of emerging automotive technology. An incident at the junction of Emory and Forest Streets illustrated the dangers of early motoring, as an automobile owned by John M. Fisher collided with a Taunton & Pawtucket electric trolley car. The result was a dramatic crash that left two injured and a scene that shocked the nearby witnesses by the extent of the damage.

Miss Gertrude Fisher, the daughter of the vehicle's owner, had taken the wheel of the car—a relatively new practice for women at the time. Despite her inexperience, she confidently approached the junction, where an electric trolley car was inbound. Accounts suggest that in an attempt to engage the brakes, Miss Fisher mistakenly activated the clutch, causing the car to lurch forward onto the tracks. The oncoming trolley had little time to stop, resulting in a catastrophic collision.

The automobile was struck with such force that it was thrown into a telegraph pole, demolishing the vehicle almost entirely. Miss Fisher was ejected through the glass windshield, suffering severe lacerations to her face and arms. According to the postcard transcription, she narrowly avoided disfigurement but faced a long recovery. The accompanying chauffeur, pinned in the wreckage, sustained internal injuries and was later taken to a sanitarium for care.

Motorman Peter Thibea and Conductor Johnson, operators of the electric car, described their attempts to avoid the crash. Thibea applied the emergency brakes and reversed the trolley's power, but it was too late. The trolley stopped just beyond the telegraph pole after impact, its occupants shaken but unharmed. Thibea and Johnson were quick to assist Miss Fisher and the chauffeur, summoning physicians to provide immediate aid.

According to the postcard penned by Mrs. B., the aftermath of the accident was somber. The message, addressed to Mrs. K., detailed the injuries sustained by the victims. Mrs. B. wrote that Gertrude faced potential permanent damage to her right hand and arm and had suffered numerous cuts. The chauffeur, while internally injured, was expected to survive. Both were recovering at a nearby sanitarium under the care of family and medical professionals.

Eyewitnesses marveled at the sheer destruction of the automobile. A new car, barely used, was rendered completely useless. Observers noted that it was a miracle that the occupants survived such a devastating collision. The electric car, though damaged, was able to return to service with minor repairs.

This accident serves as a reminder of the perils faced by early motorists, particularly as they adapted to the mechanical complexities of cars in a rapidly industrializing world. The Fisher family's misfortune also highlights the critical role of community care and emerging medical institutions, such as the sanitariums of the era, which provided respite and recovery.

The Attleboro Sun- Vol. XXI No. 274 Friday, September 2, 1910

ATTLEBORO SPRINGS & SANATORIUM

GREETINGS FROM ATTLEBORO

ATTLEBORO SPRINGS, ATTLEBORO, MASS.

"Where tired folks get rested, Where sick folks get well."
A VIEW FROM THE SANITARIUM, ATTLEBORO, MASS.

THE LAKE—ATTLEBORO SPRINGS, ATTLEBORO, MASS.

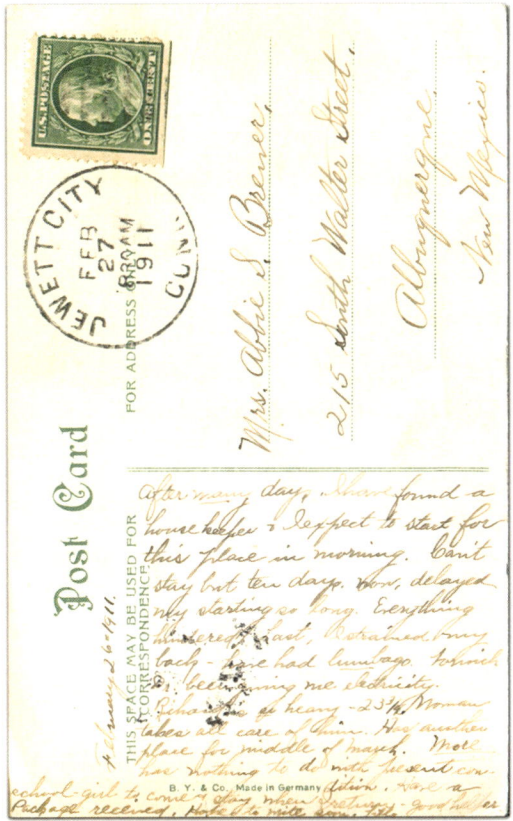

Electrifying Relief: Treating Lumbago in 1911

In a 1911 postcard, J.R.S. writes to his mother about straining his back and undergoing treatment with electricity—a relatively novel medical approach at the time. His mention of lumbago, commonly referred to as lower back pain, highlights a condition that was widespread in the early 20th century, often affecting individuals engaged in physical labor, extended travel, or general wear and tear. Medical understanding of spinal health was still developing, and treatments ranged from traditional remedies like rest and heat therapy to more experimental approaches, such as electrotherapy.

By the early 1900s, electrotherapy—particularly in the form of galvanic and faradic treatments—was gaining popularity as a means of stimulating circulation, reducing inflammation, and alleviating pain. Devices such as the "electric belt" or early electrostimulation machines were employed to deliver mild electrical currents to affected areas, often administered by physicians or physical therapists. These treatments were based on the belief that electrical stimulation could activate the nervous system, improve blood flow, and relieve muscle tension—precursors to modern transcutaneous electrical nerve stimulation (TENS) and other neuromodulation techniques.

While the efficacy of electrotherapy was debated, its appeal as a non-invasive treatment made it increasingly common. Clinics and sanatoriums promoted electricity as a cure-all for various ailments, from lumbago to nervous exhaustion. J.R.S.'s experience offers a glimpse into this era of medical experimentation, where emerging technologies blended with traditional healing methods. Though today's medicine has refined electrotherapy into more scientifically validated treatments, his letter reflects a fascinating transitional period in medical history—where innovation and anecdotal evidence often shaped treatment choices.

Bennett, Philip J. History of Electrotherapy: From Galvanic Currents to Modern TENS Therapy. Cambridge University Press, 2008.

Chalder, Andrew. "Electric Healing: The Rise of Electrotherapy in the Early 20th Century." Journal of Medical History, vol. 52, no. 4, 2010, pp. 511-532.

Fisher, Alan R. Lumbago and the Treatment of Back Pain in Medical History. Oxford University Press, 2014.

Kellaway, Peter. "The Historical Development of Electrical Stimulation of the Nervous System as a Medical Therapy." Journal of Neuroscience, vol. 5, no. 2, 1985, pp. 521–528.

Reed, Thomas C. Electrotherapy in the Progressive Era: Medical Advances and Public Skepticism. Johns Hopkins University Press, 2011.

Turner, Paul R. "Electrotherapy and the Promotion of Health in Early 20th-Century Sanatoriums." American Journal of Medical Science, vol. 128, no. 3, 1921, pp. 217-229.

ATTLEBORO SPRINGS & SANATORIUM

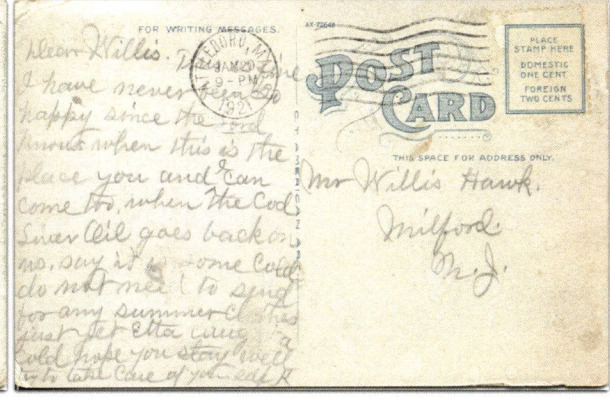

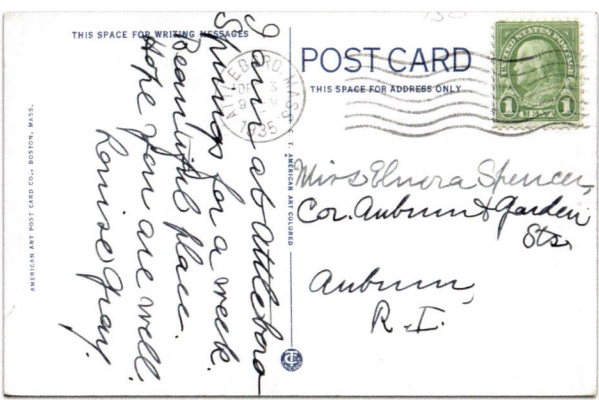

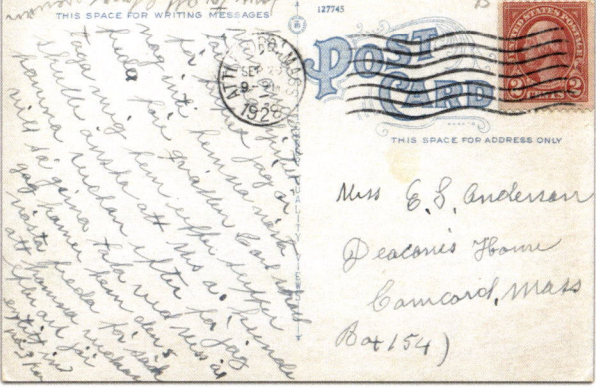

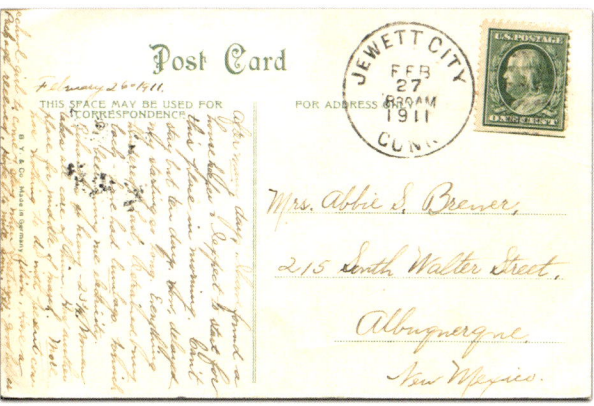

The Watson Block Fire of 1912

On October 29, 1912, a massive fire engulfed the Watson Block in Attleboro, Massachusetts, causing extensive damage and marking one of the most significant blazes in the town's history. The fire, which erupted in the early morning hours, quickly spread through the commercial district, threatening nearby businesses and leaving much of the block in ruins.

The Watson Block was a prominent commercial structure, home to various businesses, including jewelers, retailers, and professional offices. As the fire tore through the building, firefighters from Attleboro and neighboring towns battled the flames with all available resources. However, due to the rapid spread and the limitations of early 20th-century firefighting technology, their efforts were severely challenged.

According to contemporary newspaper reports, the fire was first noticed in the rear of one of the storefronts. The flames quickly moved through the structure, fueled by wooden interiors and merchandise stored inside. Within hours, the entire block was consumed, leaving behind charred remains and smoldering rubble. The loss was estimated in the tens of thousands of dollars, a considerable sum for the time

While no fatalities were reported, the disaster left a lasting impact on the local economy and prompted discussions about fire safety improvements. Many businesses lost their entire inventory, and insurance payouts only covered a fraction of the damages. The fire also underscored the need for better water pressure systems and more modern firefighting equipment in Attleboro.

In the aftermath, city officials and business owners worked to rebuild, ensuring that future structures incorporated better fire-resistant materials and updated safety measures. The Watson Block Fire of 1912 remains a significant chapter in Attleboro's history, serving as a reminder of the challenges early commercial districts faced in an era before modern fire prevention and suppression systems.

Despite the devastation, the resilience of the community was evident in the swift efforts to restore the downtown area. Within a few years, new buildings replaced those lost in the fire, contributing to the continued growth and prosperity of Attleboro

"Watson Block in Attleboro Burned Tuesday." The Daily Item [Lynn, MA], 30 Oct. 1912, p. 10.
"Serious Fire in Attleboro." Fall River Daily Evening News, 29 Oct. 1912, p. 9.
"Attleboro Fire Destroys Watson Block." Evening Times [Pawtucket, RI], 30 Oct. 1912, p. 12.
"Aftermath of Attleboro Fire: Investigation and Rebuilding Efforts." Evening Times [Pawtucket, RI], 4 Nov. 1912, p. 14.

GREETINGS FROM ATTLEBORO

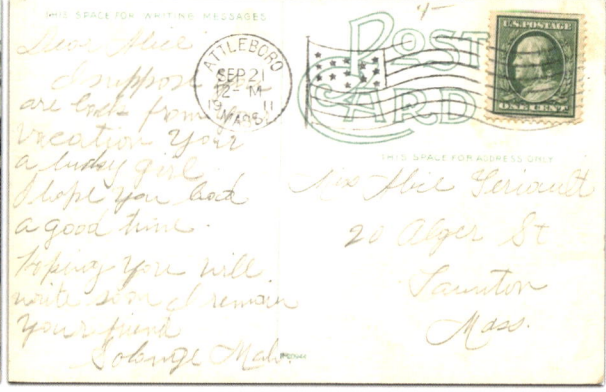

The Attleboro Public Library: A Legacy of Knowledge and Community

The Attleboro Public Library, an architectural and cultural landmark, has stood at 74 North Main Street since 1907, offering generations of residents access to knowledge, literature, and community programs. Before its establishment, the town's literary collections were housed in various buildings under the Attleboro Free Public Library Association, founded in 1885. However, it wasn't until philanthropist Joseph L. Sweet donated the land—with the condition that a library building be constructed within three years at a minimum cost of $25,000—that the town gained a dedicated public library.

The final cost of the original building far surpassed Sweet's requirement, reaching $85,000. The Boston-based architectural firm MacLean and Wright won the design competition, creating a striking Beaux-Arts structure. The Grant Brothers handled construction, bringing to life a building that featured a grand foyer, central horseshoe-shaped desk, separate reading rooms for adults and children, and a self-supporting metal book stack. The second floor housed an elegant gallery and meeting room, reinforcing the library's role as a cultural hub.

As seen in the postcard collection from the early 20th century, the library's stately façade and prominent entrance made it a beloved and frequently depicted landmark. These postcards provide a visual history of the library's evolution, showcasing its enduring presence in Attleboro's downtown area.

Over the years, the library adapted to changing needs. Between 1962 and 1974, multiple expansions added office and stack space, while a major renovation between 1992 and 1994 modernized the facility while preserving its historic charm. The latest renovation, completed in 2021, improved accessibility and expanded services.

Today, the Attleboro Public Library continues to honor its century-old mission of fostering literacy and lifelong learning. Whether through its vast collection, historical archives, or digital resources, the library remains an enduring symbol of the town's commitment to education and community enrichment—just as it was when first envisioned over a century ago.

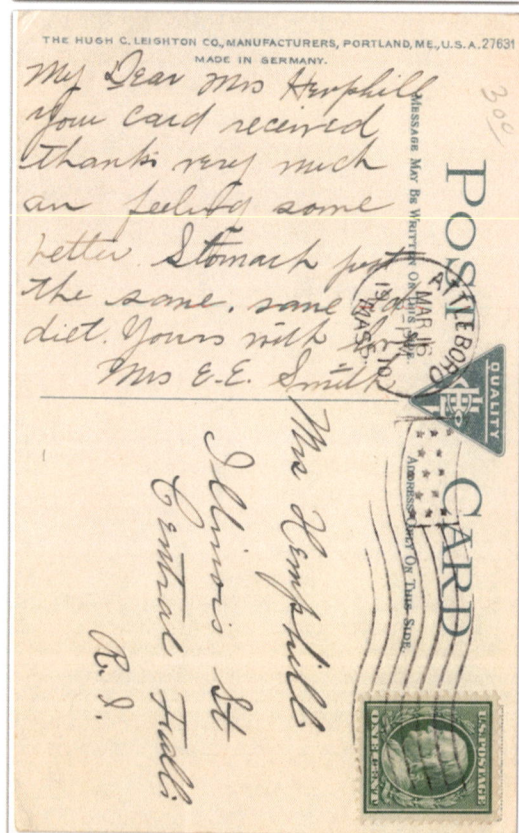

DoubleACS. History of the Attleboro Public Library. DoubleACS, 3 Nov. 2016, archive.org/details/DoubleACS_HPS_Library2016.

Attleboro Public Library. Library History. Attleboro Public Library, https://attleborolibrary.org/about/library-history/. Accessed [February 4th, 2025].

Attleboro Public Library. APL Construction Project. Attleboro Public Library, https://attleborolibrary.org/apl-construction-project/. Accessed [February 4th, 2025].

Literary Massachusetts. Attleboro Public Library. Literary Massachusetts, https://literaryma.com/places/attleboro-public-library/. Accessed [February 4th, 2025].

PUBLIC LIBRARY

THE Attleboro, Mass., Public Library was built in 1907 at a cost of $85,000. There are 22,967 books on file and more are being added. The circulation in 1921 was 119,666 volumes. The circulation in the children's room during 1921 was 33,443 volumes. The Dodgeville Branch had a circulation of 2,501 volumes in 1921, and the Hebronville Branch, 5,288. There is also a branch at the High School. The largest issue in one month was 13,439 volumes, and 823 for one day. Mrs. L. F. Spofford is the Librarian. The trustees are: J. L. Sweet, Chairman; T. E. McCaffrey, Caroline S. Holden, Mrs. Eleanor S. Carpenter, William L. King, Edwin F. Leach, Miss Edith L. Claflin, R. M. Horton and Miss Elizabeth J. Wilmarth.

Attleboro, Mass. Public Library.

Published by S. P. Clark & Co., Attleboro, Mass.

Attleboro Public Library

GREETINGS FROM ATTLEBORO

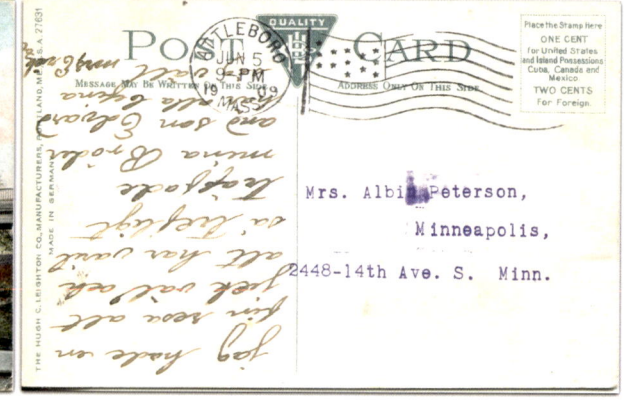

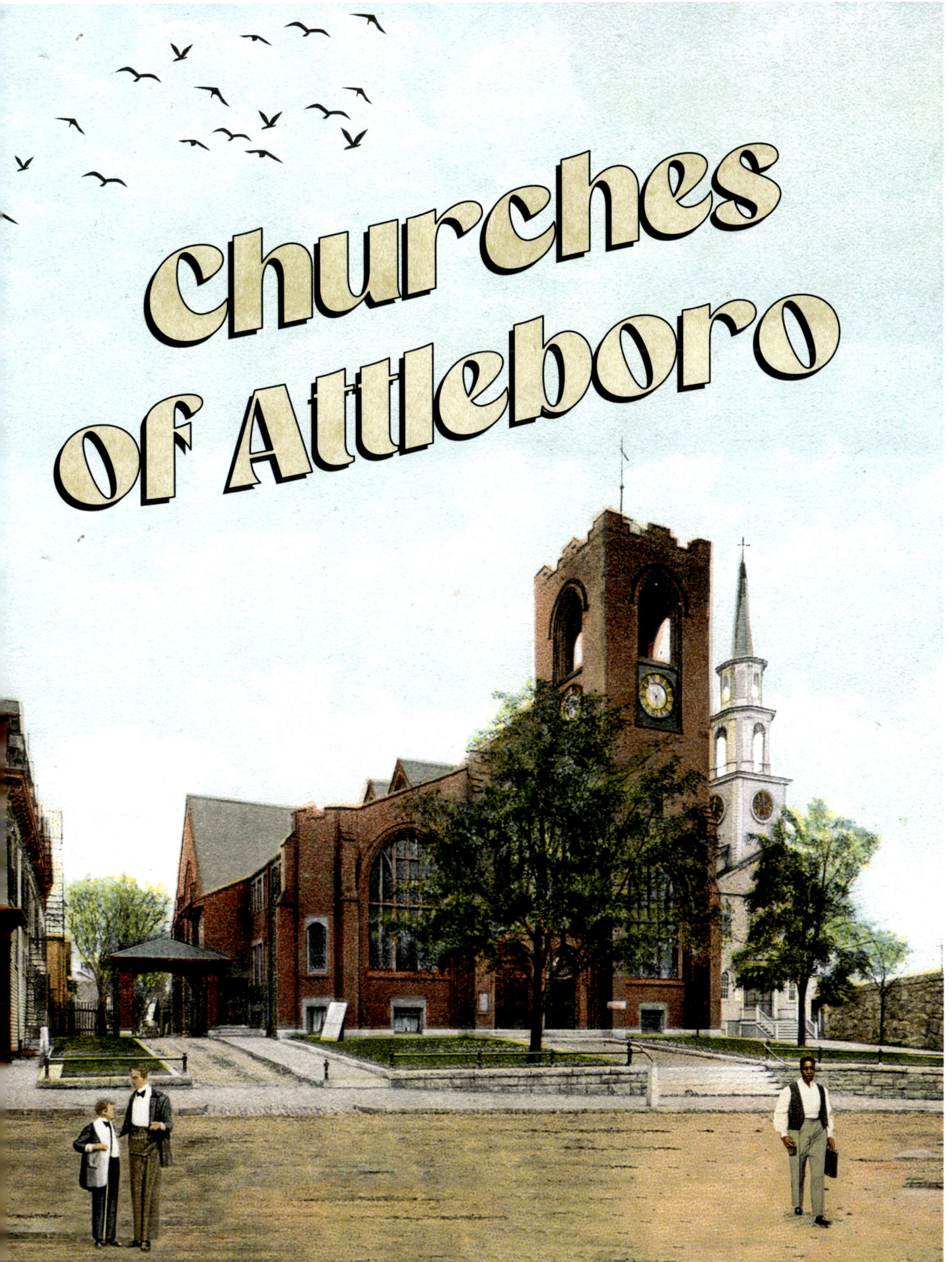

The Historic Churches of Attleboro: Faith, Community, and Legacy

The city of Attleboro, Massachusetts, has long been defined by its places of worship. From its early days as a colonial settlement to its emergence as a center of industry, churches have been at the heart of the community. Whether Congregational, Methodist, Universalist, or Catholic, these religious institutions have served as more than just places of worship; they have been centers of education, charity, and social gathering, shaping the lives of generations of Attleboro residents. Many of these churches remain active today, while others have been repurposed or lost to history, leaving behind their architectural and spiritual legacies.

The **Second Congregational Church**, founded in 1748, stands as one of the oldest religious institutions in Attleboro. It was established as part of the East Parish of Attleboro, an offshoot of the First Congregational Church in North Attleborough, which itself dates back to 1712. The first meetinghouse was constructed on land given by John Sweet, providing a place for settlers in the growing town to worship. The congregation later built a larger structure in 1825, known as the White Church, a significant landmark until its removal in 1951. The current church, erected in 1904, remains a centerpiece of downtown Attleboro. Over its long history, Second Congregational Church has witnessed shifts in religious practices and community needs, adapting to remain an integral part of the city's identity.

Methodism arrived in Attleboro later but took strong root. The **Centenary Methodist Episcopal Church**, the city's oldest Methodist congregation, was formed in 1865 under the leadership of Rev. D. H. Ela. Initially, meetings were held in private homes before the construction of the first church building in 1866. As the congregation expanded, the church played a crucial role in establishing a mission in Chartley, Norton, in 1873, further spreading Methodism in southeastern Massachusetts. The church continues its mission today as Centenary United Methodist Church, carrying forward its long-standing commitment to worship and social outreach.

The **Murray Universalist Church**, founded in 1875, has an equally fascinating history. It was named after John Murray (1741–1815), the English Methodist-turned-Universalist preacher who introduced the doctrine of universal salvation to America. In its early years, the congregation met at Union Hall, a shared space that also hosted the first Catholic services in Attleboro. By 1885, the congregation had built its own Queen Anne-style church at Main and County Streets, an architectural gem of its time. However, as the city expanded, the church moved in 1957 to a new location at 505 North Main Street, where it still serves the community. The congregation has also played a role in merging with and welcoming members from other churches, such as Pilgrim Unitarian Church, which burned down in 1926.

Catholicism in Attleboro began to take root alongside the city's industrial expansion. **St. Mary's Catholic Church**, established in

1850, was the first permanent Catholic parish in Attleboro. Before its construction, Catholic residents worshipped in private homes and at Barden's Hall, a common meeting space for early religious groups. In 1857, the congregation erected its first church building, marking an important milestone for the Catholic community. Over the years, as waves of immigrants arrived to work in Attleboro's factories, St. Mary's expanded to accommodate its growing congregation, becoming one of the city's most prominent Catholic institutions.

A few decades later, **St. Stephen's Catholic Church** was built in 1877 to serve the increasing number of French Canadian and Irish Catholic immigrants who had settled in Dodgeville and Hebronville. By the early 20th century, the church had approximately 600 members, including 350 communicants, making it a cornerstone for the French-speaking Catholic community in Attleboro. These immigrants brought with them a strong religious tradition, and the church played an essential role in preserving their culture while helping them integrate into the broader American society.

Beyond the major Protestant and Catholic congregations, Attleboro also saw the rise of Episcopalian and Christian Science movements. **All Saints Episcopal Church** emerged in the late 19th century, as the city's growing population included more Anglicans who sought a church of their own. Meanwhile, the **First Church of Christ, Scientist** began in 1919, holding services in homes before acquiring its first formal meeting space. The congregation grew steadily and, in 1927, purchased the former All Saints Episcopal Church on County Street. However, disaster struck in 1959 when a fire severely damaged the building. Undeterred, the church rebuilt at North Main Street and Wamsutta Road in 1964, adopting a New England Colonial-style design, blending modern simplicity with traditional architectural elements.

Many of these churches have weathered significant challenges, including fires, relocations, and shifts in

CHURCHES OF ATTLEBORO

cont...

demographics. Some, like Murray Universalist Church, moved locations due to the need for larger facilities or changing community needs. Others, like St. Stephen's Catholic Church, played key roles in immigrant assimilation, offering services in French and English to cater to their bilingual congregations.

The history of Attleboro's churches is not just a story of buildings and institutions but of the people who built them, worshipped in them, and sustained them through the centuries. These churches have provided education, charity, and social services, from running schools and food pantries to hosting events that bring the community together. Their architectural diversity—ranging from the classic New England meetinghouse design of Second Congregational Church to the Queen Anne and Colonial Revival styles—also reflects the evolving tastes and needs of the city's residents.

Even today, as Attleboro continues to evolve, these churches remain vital. Many have embraced modern outreach programs, interfaith dialogues, and social justice initiatives, ensuring their relevance in the 21st century. Some historic churches have merged or changed affiliations, yet they all share a common goal: to serve their community in faith and action.

From the early Congregationalists who settled in the 1700s to the Catholic and Universalist communities that flourished in the 19th and 20th centuries, the churches of Attleboro tell a story of resilience, faith, and enduring community spirit. While some buildings have been lost to time, the legacy of these religious institutions remains deeply embedded in the city's history. Whether as centers of worship, social gathering places, or historical landmarks, Attleboro's churches continue to shape the city's identity and offer a sense of continuity between the past and present.

Second Congregational Church, Attleboro, Mass.

"Attleboro Historical Sites." Attleboro Historical Preservation Society, n.d.

Daggett, John. A Sketch of the History of Attleborough: From Its Settlement to the Division. Boston: Press of Samuel Usher, 1894.

"Representative Men and Old Families of Southeastern Massachusetts." J.H. Beers & Co., 1912.

"The New England Historical and Genealogical Register." New England Historic Genealogical Society, 1904.

The Attleboro Public Library: ADA Transition Plan. Institute for Human Centered Design, 2021.

The New England Historical and Genealogical Register. Google Books, n.d. .

The New England Historical Society Archives on Attleboro Churches. New England Historical Society, n.d. .

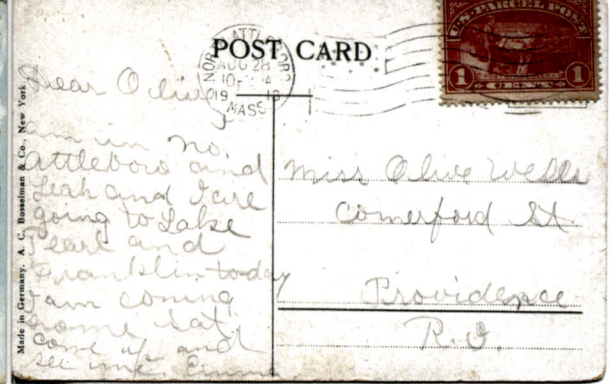

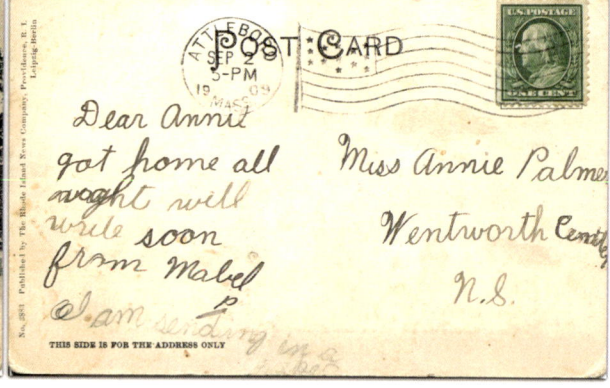

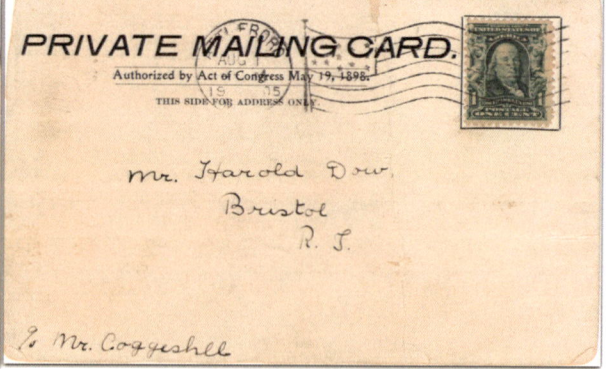

CHURCHES OF ATTLEBORO

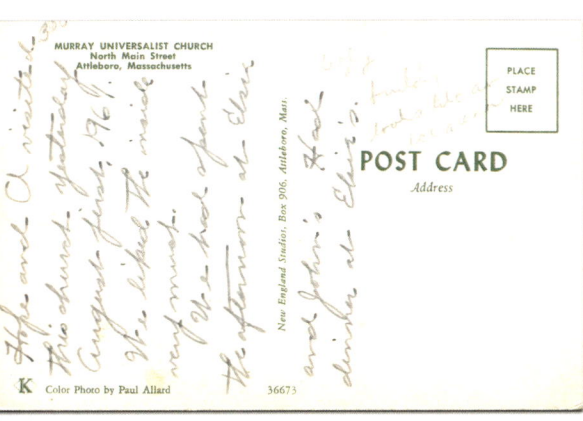

A Literary List: The Postcard as a Personal Record

Among the many postcards preserved from the early-to-mid 20th century, most carry messages sent between friends and family, brief glimpses into past lives. However, an unmailed postcard presents a unique puzzle. Unlike those adorned with addresses, postage, and transit markings, this one bears only a list of books—titles carefully noted but never sent.

Could this have been a list of books to read in the future? A note to recommend titles to a friend? Or perhaps simply a convenient scrap of paper used to jot down thoughts? The absence of a postmark suggests this postcard was never meant to travel beyond the hands of its owner, making it an artifact of personal history rather than correspondence.

The titles written on the postcard span several themes: rural life, Maine's coastal communities, family heritage, and wilderness survival. Each book, published during the mid-20th century, provides a historical snapshot of an era undergoing significant social and economic shifts.

John Gould's **Farmer Takes a Wife** and **The House That Jacob Built** reflect on life in rural Maine, documenting agricultural traditions, family structures, and the evolving landscape of small-town living. His works preserve anecdotes of self-sufficiency and craftsmanship, resonating with readers who either experienced or wished to remember a way of life that was rapidly changing.

Ruth Moore's **Spoonhandle** and Elizabeth Foster's **The Islander** similarly offer historical portrayals of Maine's coastal and island communities. At the time of their publication, these fishing villages and lakefront settlements were in transition, with tourism growing and traditional industries struggling to survive. These novels serve as literary records of these places, capturing the speech, customs, and economic concerns of the time.

Kathrene Pinkerton's **Wilderness Wife** expands this theme of self-sufficiency and adaptation, chronicling a family's survival in the Canadian wilderness. As an autobiographical account, it offers a historical perspective on frontier living, providing firsthand insights into the challenges faced by those choosing to live in isolation.

Unlike the typical postcard carrying a short message and a destination, this particular artifact offers a more intimate glimpse into someone's interests and intentions. The owner may have used it as a reminder—a to-read list capturing their curiosity about Maine's history, rural life, and human resilience. Alternatively, they may have been gathering titles to recommend to a friend, a personal form of literary exchange.

Regardless of its intended purpose, this unmailed postcard serves as a small but fascinating piece of historical evidence. It reminds us that not all postcards were sent, and not all messages needed to travel far to hold meaning. In this case, it preserves a moment of thought, a reflection of literary interests, and a quiet connection to the past.

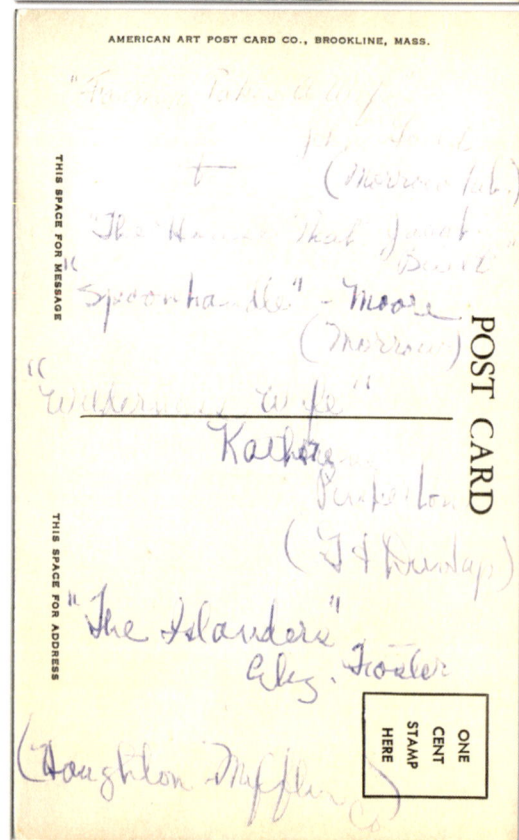

CHURCHES OF ATTLEBORO

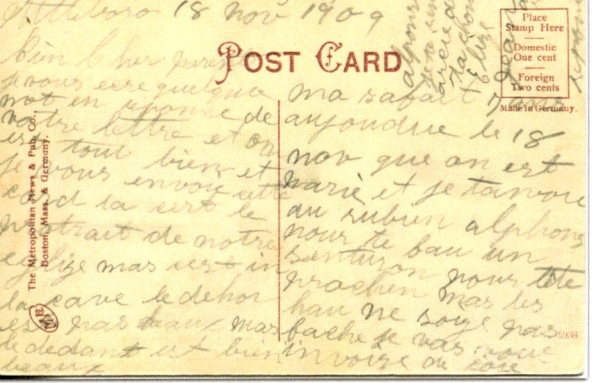

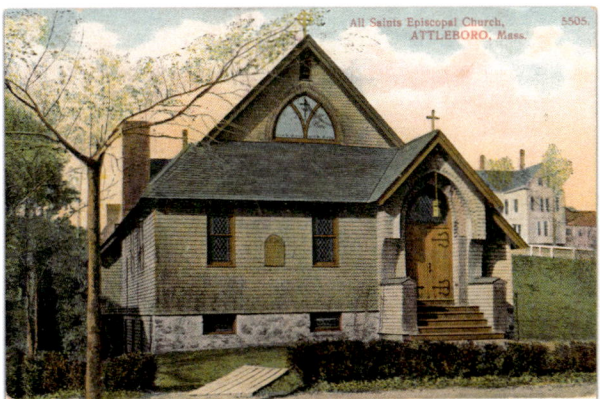
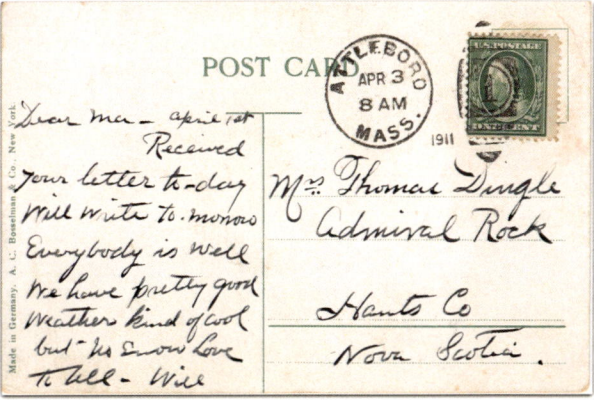

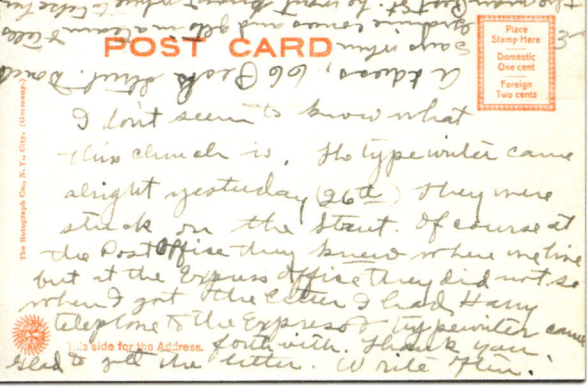

GREETINGS FROM ATTLEBORO

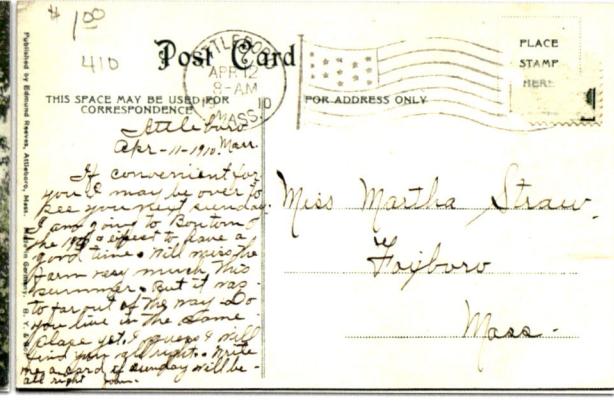

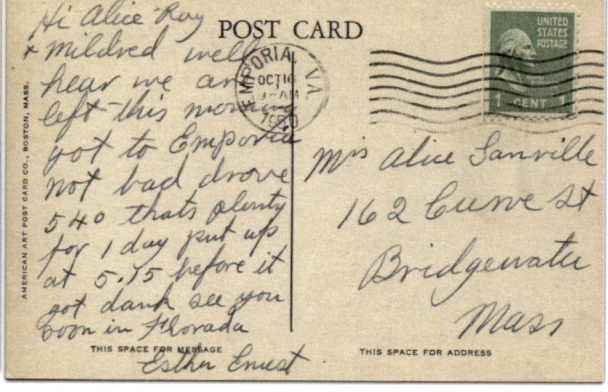
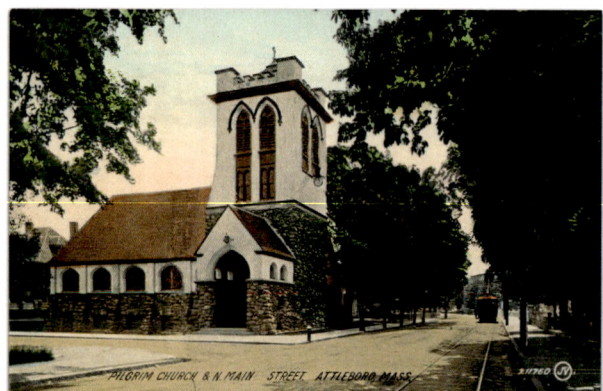
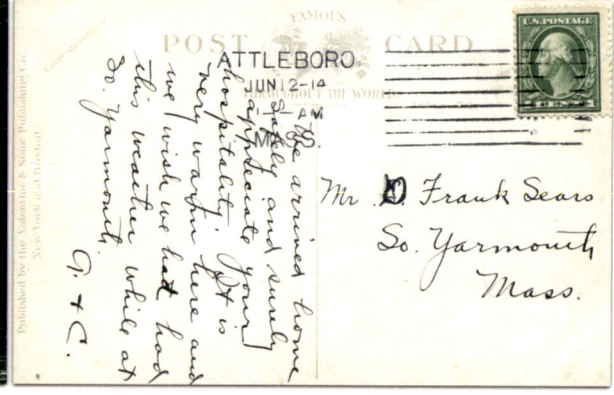

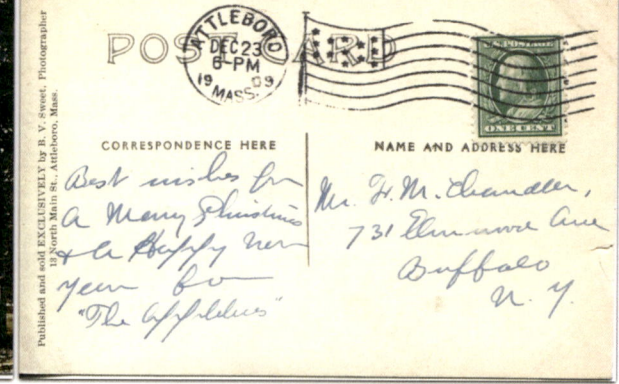

CHURCHES OF ATTLEBORO

CENTENARY METHODIST EPISCOPAL CHURCH, ATTLEBORO, MASS.

ST. JOSEPH'S CHURCH, ATTLEBORO, MASSACHUSETTS

Second Congregational Church, Attleboro, Mass.

CHURCHES OF ATTLEBORO

LA SALETTE SHRINE

La Salette Shrine: A Legacy of Hope and Reconciliation in Attleboro

Nestled in the heart of Attleboro, Massachusetts, the **National Shrine of Our Lady of La Salette** stands as a beacon of faith, healing, and tradition. From its origins as a dream of Dr. James Solomon to its transformation into one of the most cherished pilgrimage sites in New England, La Salette Shrine is an attestation to perseverance, devotion, and the power of light in times of darkness.

The Origins: Dr. Solomon's Dream

The story of La Salette in Attleboro traces back to James Solomon, a healer and visionary who gathered herbs and roots in the local woods to create remedies. Although not a medical doctor, he was widely known as "Dr. Solomon" and had grand aspirations—to build a great sanatorium where individuals could find relief from illnesses, particularly cancer.

In 1894, an engineer surveyed the grounds, and by 1901, the walls of his Solomon Sanatorium were ready to receive their massive roof. The construction, which cost $400,000, was an ambitious undertaking supported by a local businessman. On April 25, 1903, the sanatorium was officially dedicated in a grand celebration that included a parade, a band concert, and a dazzling display of 1,800 electric lights, with a searchlight projecting beams over four miles.

Despite its grandeur, financial difficulties plagued the institution. Changes in ownership became a recurring theme, and in 1919, the Methodist Church purchased the property, renaming it Attleboro Springs, inspired by the natural springs found on the grounds. The facility operated under this name until its closure in 1938.

The Arrival of the La Salette Missionaries

A new chapter began in 1942 when the Missionaries of Our Lady of La Salette acquired the property, transforming it into a major seminary. A decade later, in 1952, plans were announced for the construction of a Marian Shrine, dedicated to the Blessed Mother's apparition at La Salette, France.

The apparition, which took place on September 19, 1846, involved the Blessed Mother appearing to two shepherd children in the French Alps, delivering a message of reconciliation. She urged people to mend their ways and spread her call for faith and repentance. Inspired by this message, the Missionaries of La Salette, founded in 1852, took on the mission of sharing Mary's call to the world.

The Attleboro shrine was officially inaugurated on December 8, 1953, during the Feast of the Immaculate Conception, marking the beginning of the Marian Year declared by Pope Pius XII. The opening celebration featured fireworks, an outdoor nativity scene, and a gathering of over 5,000 people.

The Christmas Festival of Lights and National Recognition

What started as a modest outdoor nativity scene has since grown into the renowned Christmas Festival of Lights, attracting over 500,000 pilgrims annually. Featuring over 300,000 dazzling lights, the festival transforms the shrine into a winter wonderland, drawing visitors from across the country. However, the shrine faced a tragic setback on November 5, 1999, when a devastating fire destroyed the historic Solomon Sanatorium. Undeterred, the La Salette community rebuilt, and on September 19, 2000, a new Shrine Church of Our Lady of La Salette was dedicated, once again reaffirming the site's mission of faith and renewal.

In 2003, the shrine received national recognition when the U.S. Conference of Catholic Bishops officially designated it as the National Shrine of Our Lady of La Salette.

A Legacy of Healing and Reconciliation

Throughout its history, the site of La Salette Shrine in Attleboro has embodied themes of struggle, hope, and healing. From Dr. Solomon's ambitious dream to the mission of the La Salette priests, the land has served as a place of comfort and light, guiding generations of believers on their spiritual journeys. Today, it continues to welcome visitors, offering a peaceful sanctuary for prayer, reflection, and celebration. For those seeking inspiration, solace, or simply the beauty of a winter spectacle, La Salette Shrine remains a cherished landmark, a symbol of faith that endures through time.

LA SALETTE SHRINE

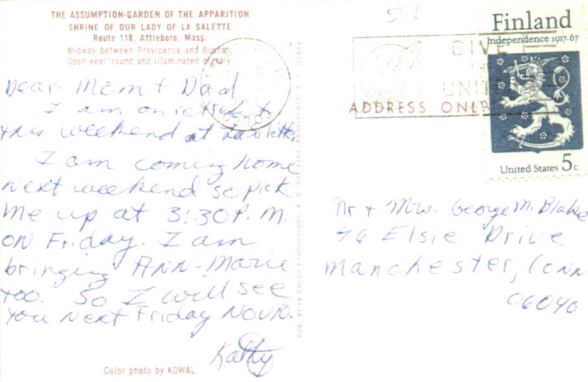

SANCTUAIRE　　LA SALETTE　　SHRINE

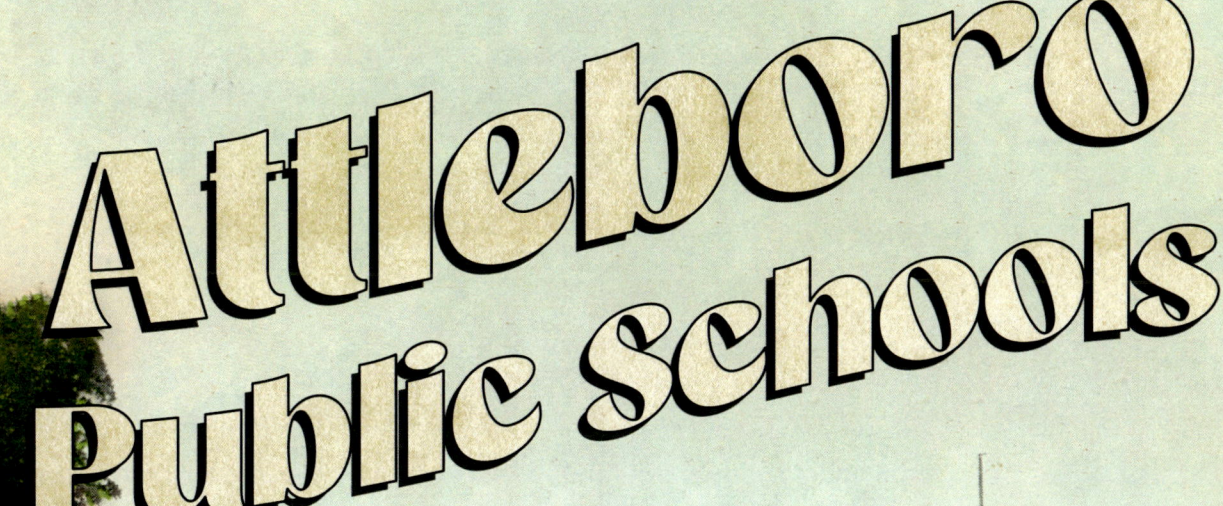

Attleboro Public Schools

The Evolution of Attleboro Public Schools

Education has long been a cornerstone of Attleboro's growth, shaping the city's development from its early days as a collection of small district schools to the modern institutions of the 20th century. The city's commitment to education dates back to the colonial era, when Massachusetts laws mandated public schooling. In the 19th century, Attleboro's schools were scattered across multiple districts, with small, one-room schoolhouses serving students of all ages in mixed classrooms. These early schools provided a basic education, but they struggled with irregular attendance, teacher shortages, and limited resources. By the late 1800s, reforms in Massachusetts led to the consolidation of these district schools, setting the stage for a more structured public education system.

As Attleboro entered the 20th century, the demand for formalized secondary education grew, spurred by industrial expansion and a changing workforce. The city's first high school was housed in a temporary location in the Straw Shop before a dedicated high school building was established. In this era, high schools offered classical subjects like Latin and rhetoric, but they also adapted to the needs of a growing industrial economy by introducing vocational and technical training.

By the 1930s, Attleboro had firmly committed to developing a strong public school system, recognizing that education was essential not just for higher learning but for preparing students for the city's booming industries. The Attleboro Jewelry Trade School, founded in 1934, reflected this shift. As the city became a national leader in jewelry manufacturing, the school provided hands-on training for students entering the trade, a model that foreshadowed the rise of technical and vocational programs in later decades.

The mid-20th century saw a dramatic shift in Attleboro's educational landscape. With a post-war population boom and increasing emphasis on structured learning, the city needed larger, more modern schools. One significant addition was Willett Elementary School, constructed in 1941, which was part of a broader trend of replacing aging buildings with new facilities better suited for growing class sizes.

During the 1950s and 1960s, the junior high school model transitioned into the more familiar middle school structure, allowing for a more specialized curriculum tailored to pre-teen students. Schools in this era emphasized both academic subjects and practical skills, reflecting a national movement toward comprehensive education. The construction of new schools during this time ensured that Attleboro students had access to science labs, libraries, and extracurricular programs that had been absent in earlier decades.

High school education in Attleboro continued to evolve throughout the 20th century. The former Attleboro High School, which appears in many postcards from this era, was central to the city's academic and social life. Its architecture, representative of early-20th-century school design, symbolized an era when

SANFORD STREET SCHOOL, ATTLEBORO, MASS.

public schools were expanding both in physical space and in curriculum. Students of the 1950s and 1960s experienced a school environment that balanced traditional subjects with emerging fields like business education, home economics, and industrial arts.

By the 1970s, Attleboro's school system had fully transitioned into a modern educational model, with larger schools, expanded programming, and a commitment to preparing students for a broad range of careers. The city continued to invest in its schools, ensuring that students had access to evolving technologies and educational advancements.

Many of the images featured in this postcard collection capture Attleboro's schools as they stood in the mid-20th century—buildings that served generations of students before being replaced or renovated. The former high school, which was a defining presence in the community for much of the 20th century, was eventually replaced with a state-of-the-art facility in 2021, marking a new chapter in the city's educational history.

From small one-room schoolhouses to the large, modern institutions of the 20th century, Attleboro's schools reflect the city's ongoing commitment to education. The transition from scattered district schools to a centralized system was driven by the needs of a growing population and an evolving economy. While the buildings and teaching methods have changed, the goal has remained the same—to provide quality education and opportunities for Attleboro's students. These postcards serve as a visual history of that journey, preserving the legacy of the schools that shaped the city's past and continue to influence its future.

Spatcher, Dyanne. "History of the Attleboro Public Schools." YouTube, uploaded by DoubleACS,

ATTLEBORO PUBLIC SCHOOLS

Attleboro High School. Attleboro, Mass.

HIGH SCHOOL, ATTLEBORO, MASS.

Senior High School, Attleboro, Mass.

GREETINGS FROM ATTLEBORO

RICHARDSON SCHOOL, ATTLEBORO, MASS.

Grammar School, Attleboro, Mass.

Working Conditions and Job Insecurity in Early 20th Century Attleboro

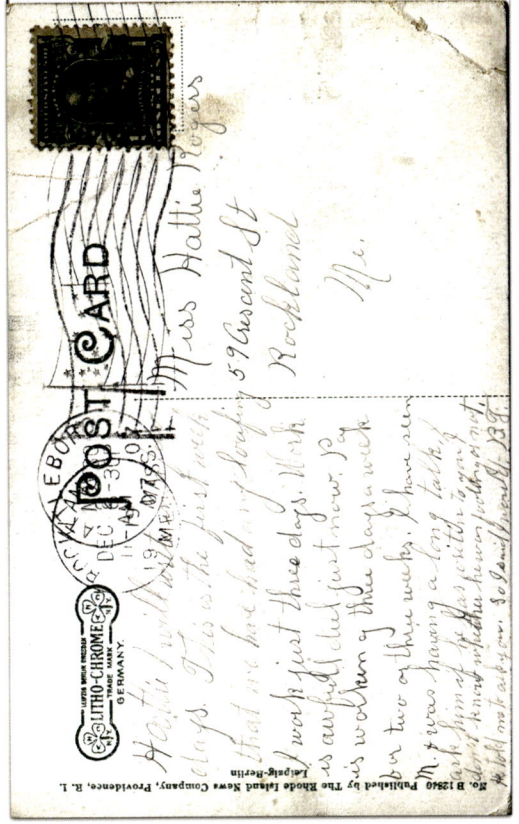

In the early 20th century, Attleboro, Massachusetts, was a bustling industrial hub, known primarily for its jewelry manufacturing. However, despite the town's economic growth, many workers faced job insecurity and inconsistent employment. A 1907 postcard from an Attleboro resident to a friend in Rockland, Maine, captures the uncertain nature of work at the time, lamenting that employment had slowed to just three days a week. This firsthand account reflects a larger trend of economic instability that affected workers across industries.

By the early 1900s, Attleboro had established itself as a center for manufacturing, particularly in the jewelry trade. The town was home to several factories producing watch chains, brooches, rings, and other fine accessories. Alongside jewelry, other industries flourished, including metalworking, textile production, and small-scale manufacturing. Despite this industrial expansion, employment was not always steady.

Workers often faced underemployment rather than outright unemployment, meaning they might work only a few days per week due to fluctuating demand for goods. Unlike today's labor protections, there were few safety nets—no unemployment benefits, minimum wage laws, or guaranteed work hours. The lack of regulations meant that factory owners could adjust schedules based on economic conditions, leaving workers with unpredictable incomes.

The early 20th century was marked by periodic economic downturns, including the Panic of 1907, which led to financial instability across the country. Industrial cities like Attleboro were particularly vulnerable to such crises, as demand for luxury goods like jewelry declined sharply. As factory orders slowed, workers bore the brunt of these economic swings. Some were laid off entirely, while others were placed on reduced schedules—working just two or three days a week.

For many families, seasonal employment was a reality. Jewelry and metalwork production often slowed during economic downturns, while the textile industry, another major employer in the region, also experienced fluctuations based on material availability and trade conditions. Workers had to find alternative means of support, such as taking on temporary jobs, farming, or relying on family members for financial help.

To cope with economic uncertainty, many Attleboro families relied on multiple sources of income. Women and children frequently contributed by working in domestic service, sewing, or small manufacturing shops. Some families took in boarders to earn extra money, while others grew their own food to reduce expenses.

Despite these hardships, Attleboro's workers remained resilient. The early 1900s saw the beginnings of labor organizing, with employees pushing for better wages and more stable working conditions. While unions were still in their infancy, workers were becoming increasingly aware of the need for protections against exploitative labor practices.

The postcard from 1907 serves as a reminder of the precarious nature of industrial work at the time. While Attleboro's factories provided economic opportunities, the lack of stability meant that many workers faced ongoing financial stress. Today, the legacy of Attleboro's industrial workforce endures, offering insight into the struggles and resilience of the working class during a transformative era in American labor history.

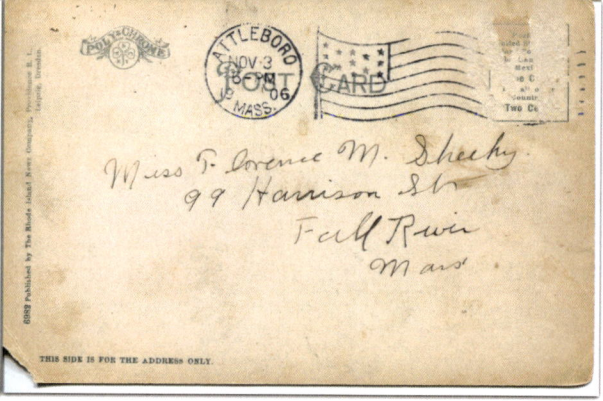

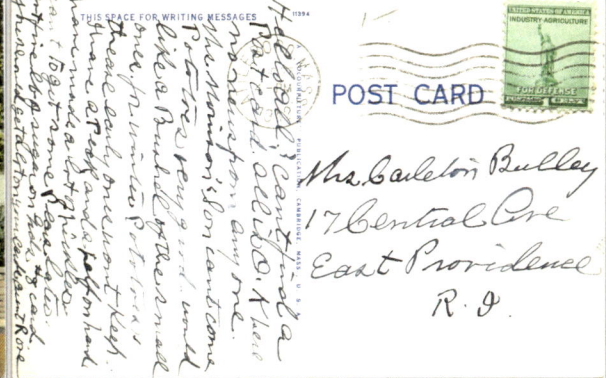

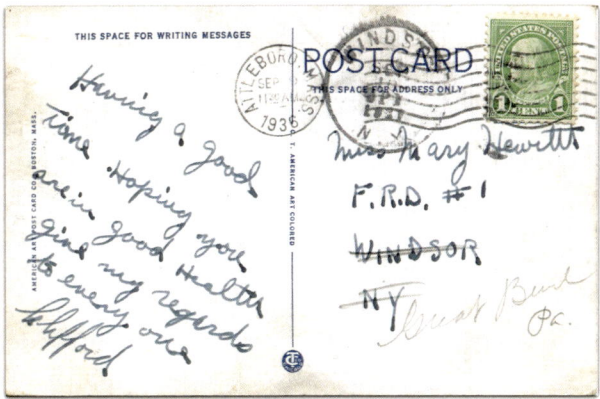

A Frightful Trolley Crash in 1907: A Close Call for S.E. Coggeshall

In the summer of 1907, Attleboro was a growing industrial town, its streets bustling with factory workers, families, and the newly expanding trolley system. The electric streetcars had become the backbone of local transportation, linking neighborhoods and leisure destinations like Taunton Park. However, progress came with risks, as tragically demonstrated by the Briggs Corner trolley crash on the evening of August 8, 1907.

A Taunton & Pawtucket streetcar packed with passengers slammed into the back of another car that had stopped just around a bend to let off a passenger. With the air brakes rendered useless—later determined to be the result of deliberate tampering—the second car was unable to stop in time, crashing with terrifying force. Several passengers were thrown into the road, and at least 10 people sustained serious injuries, including Miss Laura Anthony, who was knocked unconscious, and Miss Sadie Wetherell, whose foot was trapped by the bent iron dasher. The accident, which could have been even deadlier, sent shockwaves through the town, and authorities launched an immediate investigation to find the culprit responsible for tampering with the brakes.

Among the passengers that evening was Miss S.E. Coggeshall, who later wrote about her experience in a postcard addressed to a friend in Bristol, Rhode Island. *"I was not hurt but quite well shaken up,"* she recounted, adding that *"many were injured, but I was lucky to be seated three rows from the back."* Her words, captured in a simple note, preserve a firsthand account of a terrifying night in Attleboro's history.

The Briggs Corner crash was a stark reminder of the dangers that came with modern transportation. While the trolley system connected the community like never before, it also introduced new vulnerabilities. The investigation confirmed that the air brakes had been intentionally disengaged by an unknown passenger—a criminal act that endangered hundreds of lives. Though the perpetrator was never identified, the incident led to stricter safety protocols for trolley operations.

Electric Street Car

"Collision at Briggs Corner: 10 Injured." The Attleboro Sun, vol. XVIII, no. 244, 9 Aug. 1907, p. 1..

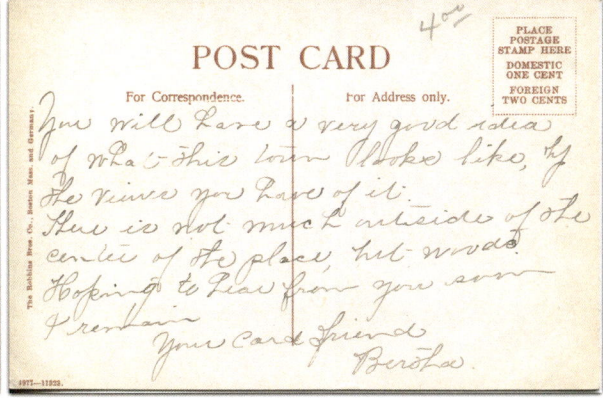

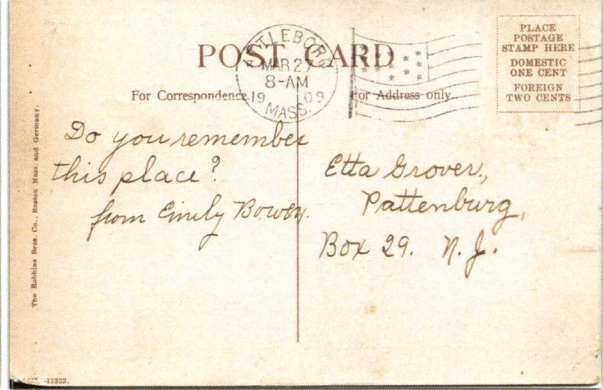

GREETINGS FROM ATTLEBORO

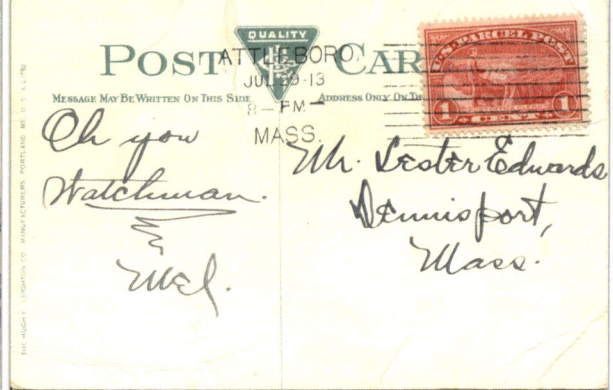

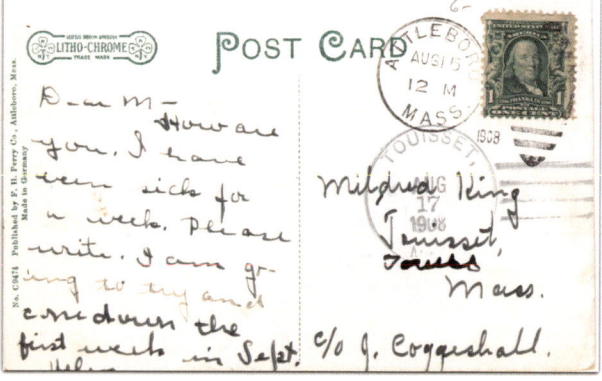

GREETINGS FROM ATTLEBORO

Attleboro, Mass. Capron Park Casino.

Capron Park Casino, Attleboro, Mass.

CAPRON PARK

Capron Park: A Century of Community and History in Attleboro

Capron Park, one of Attleboro's most cherished landmarks, has served as a center for recreation, relaxation, and community engagement for over a century. Established in the early 1900s, the park was made possible through the generosity of the Capron family, who donated the land in memory of Dennis Capron. The park has since evolved, preserving its historical significance while adapting to modern recreational needs, including the beloved Capron Park Zoo, which continues to attract visitors today.

Capron Park officially opened to the public on September 2, 1901, on land that had once been part of the Dennis Capron farm. This estate, which spanned 110 acres, was integral to early Attleboro, later transforming into one of the city's most attractive residential areas. The park was designed as a place where families could gather and enjoy the outdoors, marking a pivotal moment in Attleboro's efforts to create public green spaces.

Among the park's early features was the Perry Memorial Casino, an elegant structure originally built as an ice cream parlor, which quickly became a social hub for visitors. In addition to the Casino, the park received landscaping enhancements, including gardens, a decorative fountain, and a grand entrance gateway, all of which added to its charm and made it a central gathering spot for residents.

By the 1910s and 1920s, Capron Park had become a focal point for city events and leisure activities. Open green spaces were utilized for community gatherings, concerts, and celebrations, strengthening its reputation as an essential part of the Attleboro community. The city's investment in the park during these years signified a broader movement to create public recreation spaces that were accessible to all.

In the late 1930s, the city expanded the park's amenities with the addition of the Capron Park Zoo, which would later become one of the most notable attractions in the region. Originally a modest collection of animals, the zoo grew into an institution that provided education and entertainment to generations of families. Today, it continues to serve as an integral part of the park, offering conservation programs and interactive exhibits.

As the city of Attleboro expanded, so did Capron Park's facilities. Over the years, playgrounds, walking paths, picnic areas, and sports facilities were added, ensuring that the park remained a vital part of the community. Now, well over a century since its founding, Capron Park remains a treasured space where history meets modern recreation, standing as a testament to Attleboro's dedication to preserving its green spaces for future generations.

Attleboro Historical Sites Booklet. Attleboro Historical Commission, n.d.
Representative Men and Old Families of Southeastern Massachusetts. J.H. Beers & Co., 1912.
Bonneville, Victor, and Paula T. Sollitto. Attleboro. Arcadia Publishing, 1999.

CAPRON PARK

View from Shelter, Capron Park, Attleboro, Mass.

DUCK POND, CAPRON PARK, ATTLEBORO, MASSACHUSETTS 1479

Capron Park, Attleboro, Mass.

GREETINGS FROM ATTLEBORO

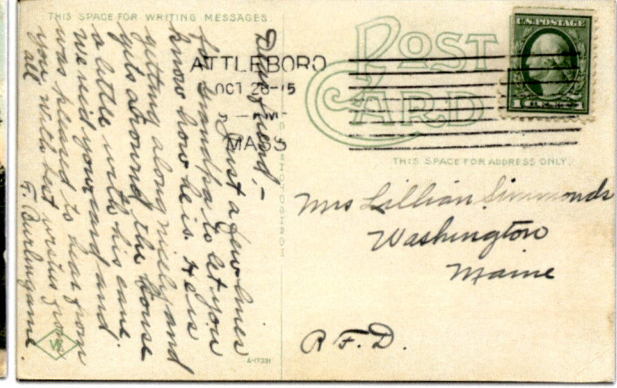

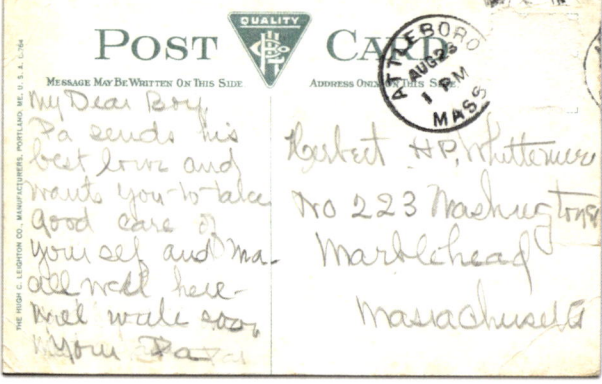

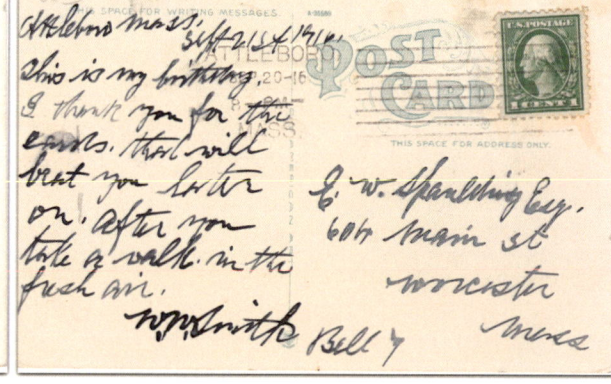

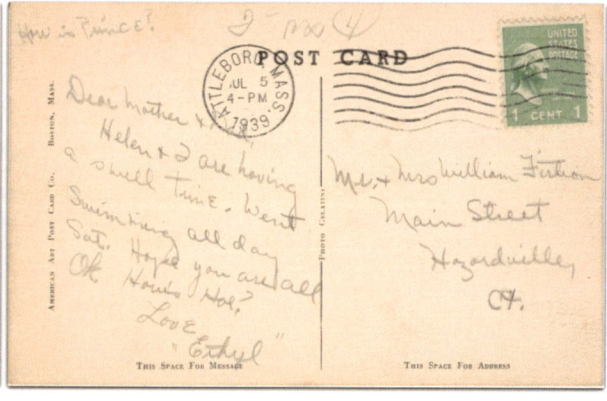

CAPRON PARK

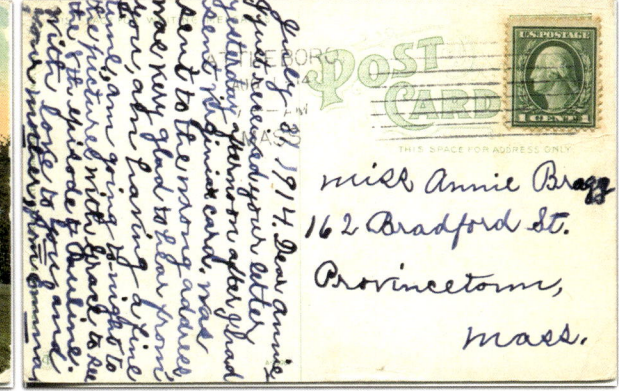

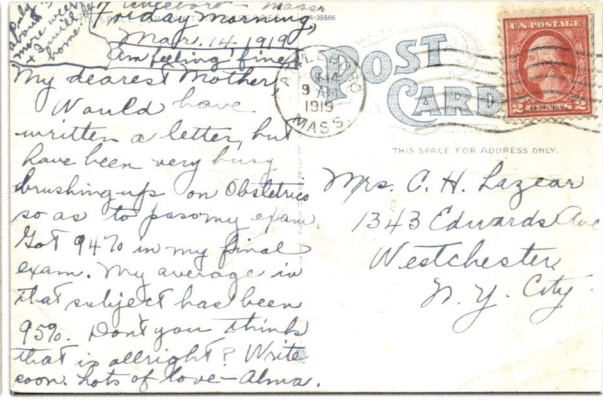

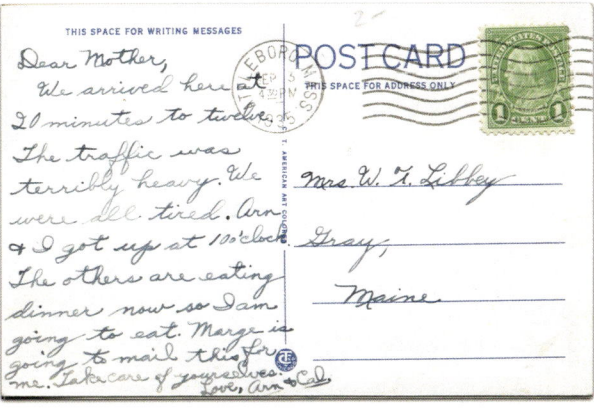

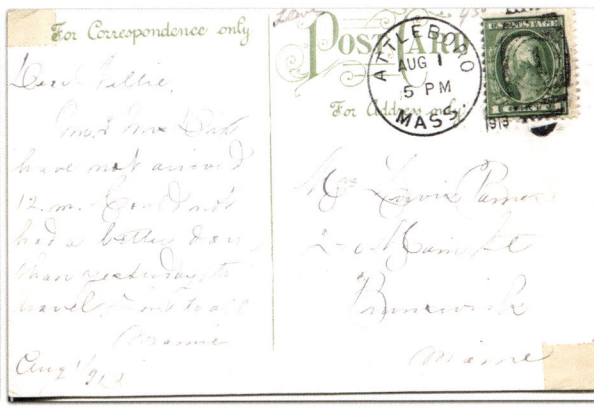

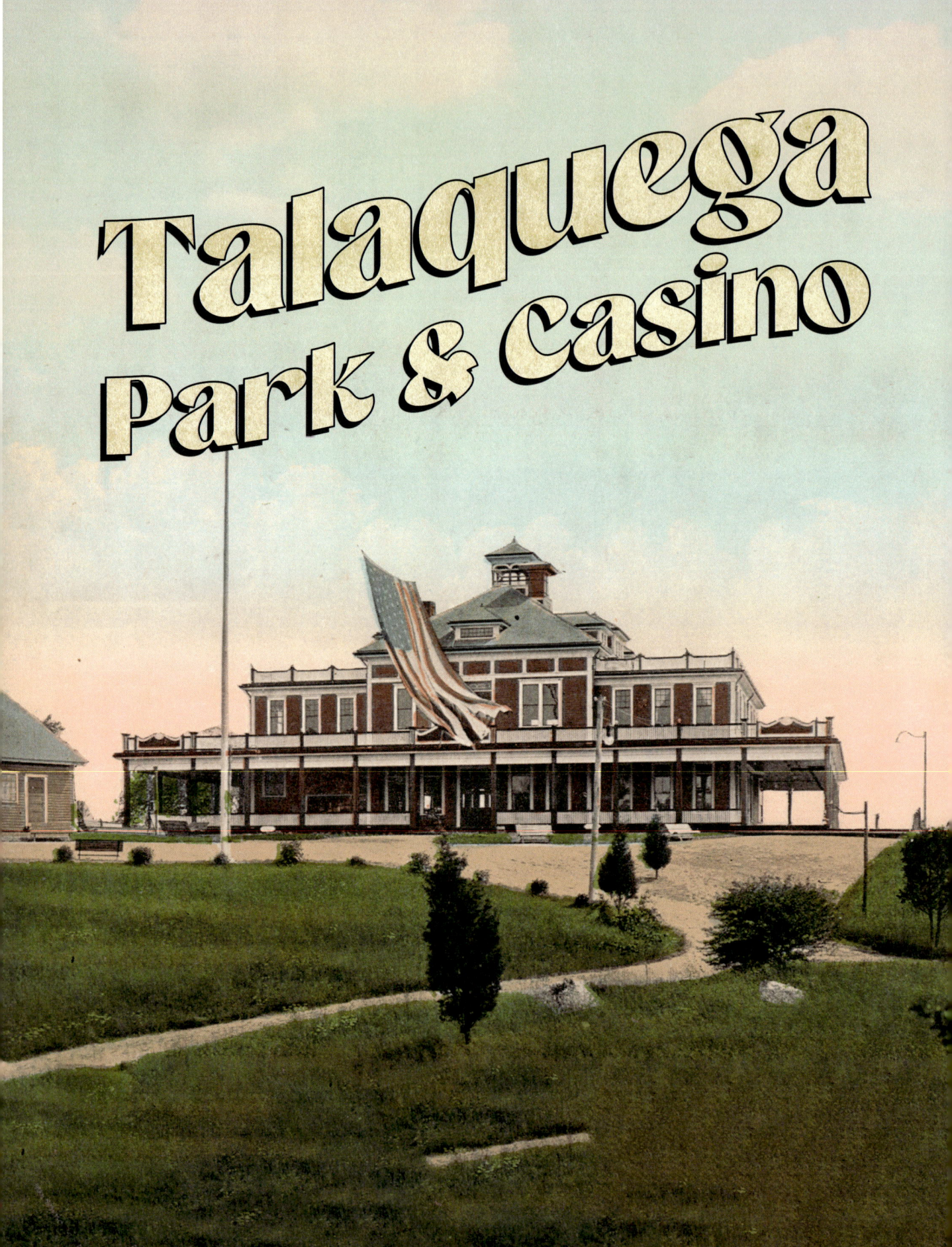

TALAQUEGA PARK & CASINO

GREETINGS FROM ATTLEBORO

Talaquega Park, A Forgotten Amusement Park in Attleboro

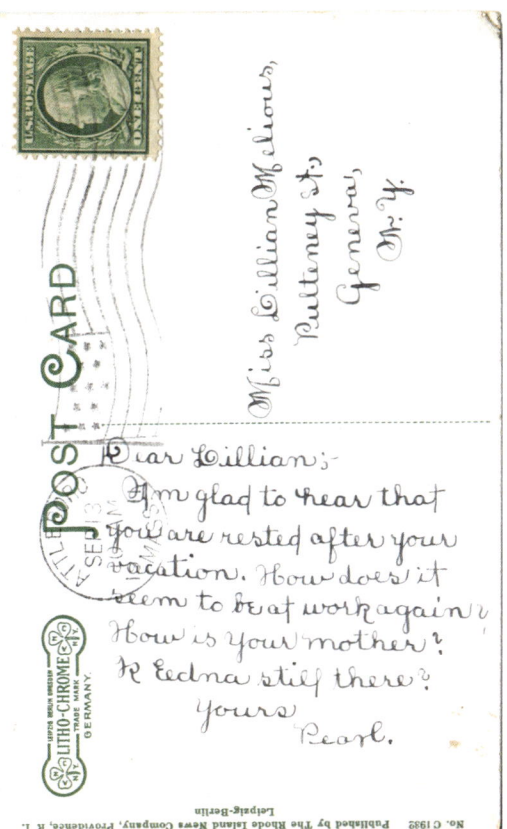

In the early 1900s, amusement parks were rapidly expanding throughout New England, often built along trolley lines to encourage ridership. Talaquega Park in Attleboro, Massachusetts, was one such establishment, offering entertainment and leisure for the local community. Developed as a response to the growing demand for accessible recreational spaces, the park was an ambitious project that briefly flourished before fading into history.

Talaquega Park opened in the early 1900s as an amusement destination along the Bristol County Electric Railway. Investors, recognizing the success of similar trolley parks like Rocky Point in Rhode Island, envisioned Talaquega as a major entertainment venue. In 1902, plans were drawn for a two-story casino featuring a café, waiting rooms, a dance pavilion, and an entertainment space, costing an estimated $20,000.

The park offered a variety of attractions, including a five-star restaurant, a four-lane bowling alley, and vaudeville performances. Families could enjoy nature walks through the wooded landscape, rent rowboats for a relaxing afternoon, or watch circus performances during the summer. Colonel Randall A. Harrington, a former Broadway figure and a major investor in New England amusement parks, was instrumental in Talaquega's development. His promotional efforts brought in famous vaudeville acts traveling between Boston and Rhode Island.

Despite its early success, the park's decline was inevitable. The increasing popularity of automobiles, the downfall of the trolley system, and the financial struggles brought on by World War I led to a decrease in visitors. By 1917, Harrington sold Talaquega Park to Bristol County, and in 1919, the site was repurposed as the Bristol County Tuberculosis Hospital.

The hospital served as a critical medical facility for the region, offering care for tuberculosis patients until the disease was largely eradicated by the 1950s. The site was later converted into a nursing home, operating under the name Bristol County Nursing Home until 2001, when it was shut down due to financial constraints and safety concerns. The property remained vacant until Grace Baptist Church purchased it in 2003, undertaking significant renovations, including asbestos removal and roof repairs.

While Talaquega Park is now a distant memory, its history remains a fascinating chapter in Attleboro's development. What once served as a bustling amusement park later became a place of healing, reflecting the changing needs of the community. Today, its legacy endures through historical records and the lingering presence of structures that once made up this forgotten piece of Attleboro's past.

"Bristol County Tuberculosis Hospital." Bristol County, Massachusetts, digitized by Google.
"Plans for Talaquega Park Casino Announced." Taunton Gazette, 1902.
"Talaquega Park and Its Evolution," Attleboro Historical Society Archives.
"Trolley Parks and the Rise of Amusement Centers," New England Historical Review.

GREETINGS FROM ATTLEBORO

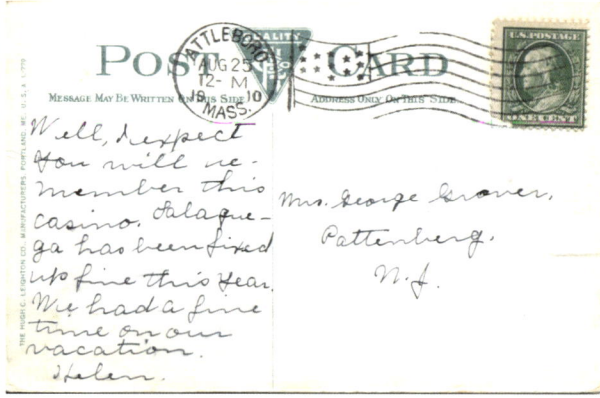

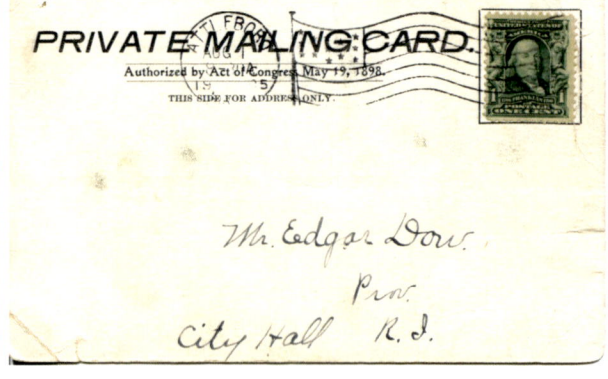

TALAQUEGA PARK & CASINO

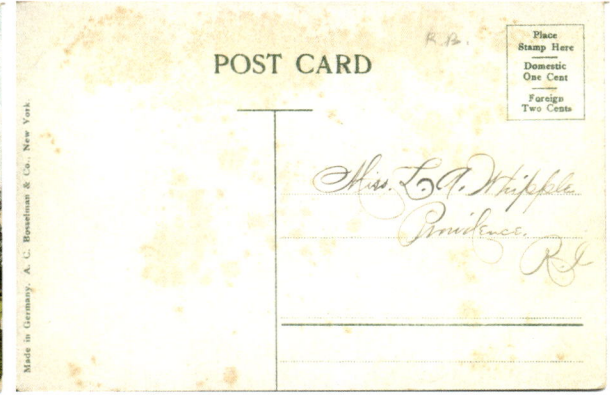

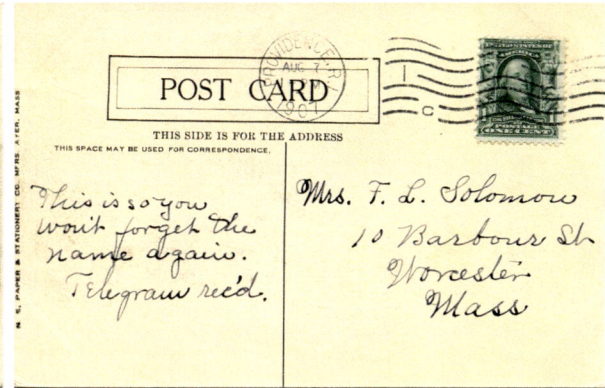

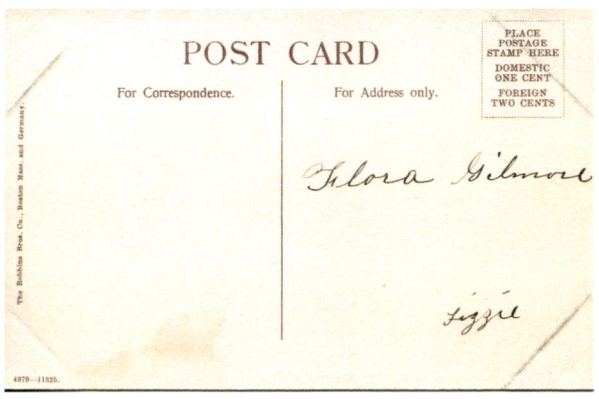

Highland Country Club of Attleboro

Highland Country Club, nestled in Attleboro, Massachusetts, boasts a rich history dating back to its establishment in 1901. The club originated when Clarence Watson generously donated his farm for the creation of this esteemed institution. Over the years, it evolved into a prominent venue featuring a nine-hole golf course, driving range, pro-shop, clubhouse, and practice areas. Members cherished the meticulously maintained greens and the vibrant social events hosted within its elegant clubhouse.

However, after 117 years of operation, the club faced financial challenges and filed for bankruptcy in 2018, leading to its closure. Recognizing the site's potential for community enrichment, the City of Attleboro acquired the 93-acre property later that year, transforming it into what is now known as Highland Park. This transition ensured the preservation of the land for public recreational use, allowing residents and visitors to enjoy its rolling hills, diverse tree species, and serene ponds

Today, Highland Park offers a tranquil retreat with paved walking paths, remnants of sand traps, and benches that hint at its storied past as a golf course. The park's landscape provides a haven for birdwatching and leisurely strolls, inviting all to experience the natural beauty and historical significance of this cherished community asset.

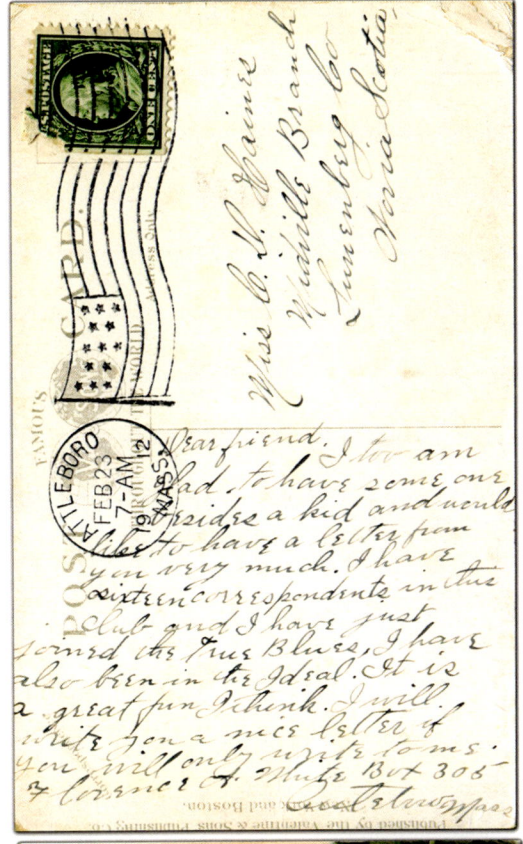

Friends of Attleboro Recreation. Doran Family Highland Park Fund. 2018, https://foar-attleboro.com/doran-family-highland-park-fund/. Accessed 18 Mar. 2025.

"Highland Park – Attleboro." Trails and Walks RI, 28 Apr. 2019, https://trailsandwalksri.wordpress.com/2019/04/28/highland-park-attleboro/. Accessed 18 Mar. 2025..

The Vista at Mechanics Pond: A Historical Perspective

Nestled in the heart of Attleboro, Massachusetts, Mechanics Pond is a picturesque location rich in industrial history. Over the centuries, it has been a vital part of the town's economic and infrastructural development. Featuring the Mechanics Dam and the old stone bridge, "The Vista" pictured on these postcards, offers a glimpse into the past, showcasing the intersection of natural beauty and industrial innovation.

Mechanics Pond has long been a focal point for industry in Attleboro. In the early 18th century, the land surrounding the pond was utilized for ironworks, a crucial industry at the time. Robert Saunderson, a Boston merchant, was among the first to establish a forge near the site, building a home modeled after English architecture. By 1712, the forge had changed hands, being sold to Robert Lightfoot, another prominent merchant. The presence of ironworks near the pond highlights its role as an industrial power source long before Attleboro became a manufacturing hub.

Before ironworks, the site housed grist and sawmills, further solidifying its status as a center for resource processing. The transition from small-scale milling operations to full-fledged manufacturing plants underscores the industrial evolution of Attleboro.

The Mechanics Dam was constructed to regulate water flow, ensuring a steady supply for the mills and forges operating along the pond. Dams like this were essential to early industrial towns, where waterpower was the lifeblood of manufacturing. The controlled release of water enabled consistent mill operation, supporting the growth of Attleboro's economy. As technology advanced and steam power replaced water-driven industry, the significance of the dam diminished. However, it remains a historical landmark, symbolizing a time when water-powered mills dominated the landscape.

The old stone bridge at Mechanics Pond is another remarkable feature of "The Vista." Likely constructed during the mid-to-late 19th century, the bridge served as a crucial transportation link, allowing goods and workers to move efficiently between mills and markets. Built from sturdy stone masonry, the bridge has withstood the test of time, a testament to 19th-century engineering prowess.

Bridges like this were instrumental in shaping New England's industrial landscape, connecting communities and facilitating commerce. While the bridge may no longer serve as a primary transport route, its presence near Mechanics Pond offers a tangible link to Attleboro's rich industrial past.

Daggett, John. A Sketch of the History of Attleborough, from Its Settlement to the Division. Press of Samuel Usher, 1894.

"Attleboro Historical Sites." Attleboro Historical Preservation Society, PDF file.

"Representative Men and Old Families of Southeastern Massachusetts." J. H. Beers & Co., 1912

GREETINGS FROM ATTLEBORO

 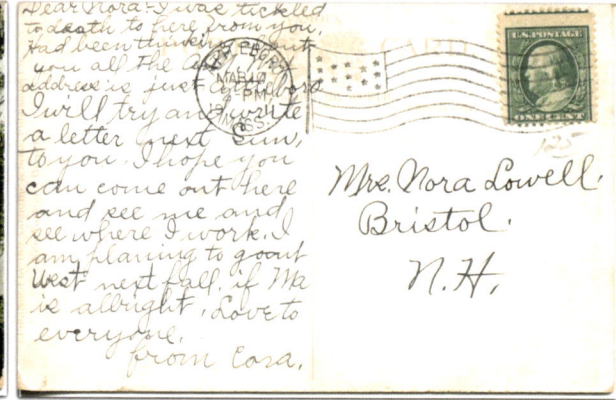

 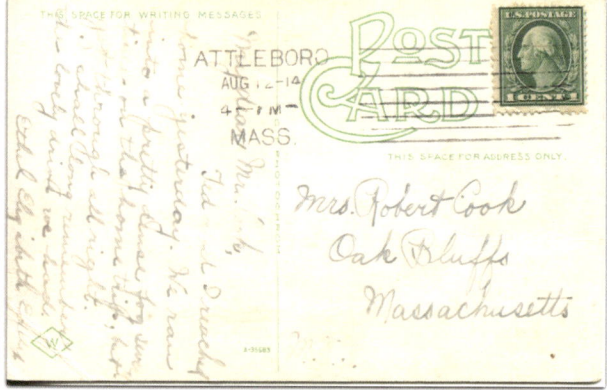

 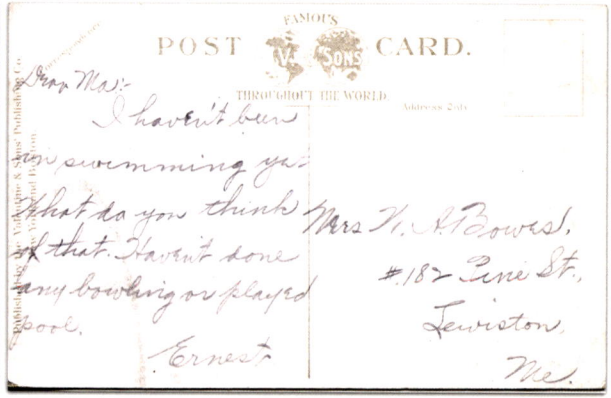

MECHANICS POND

 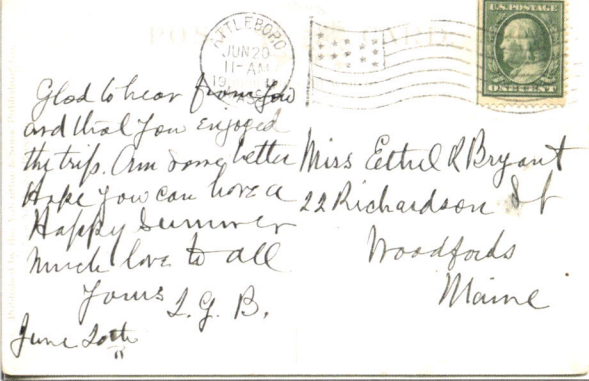

 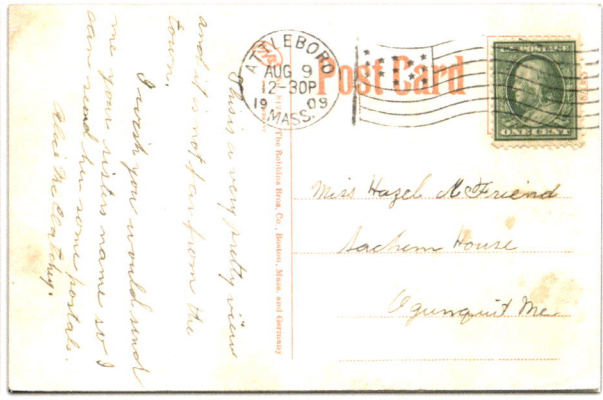

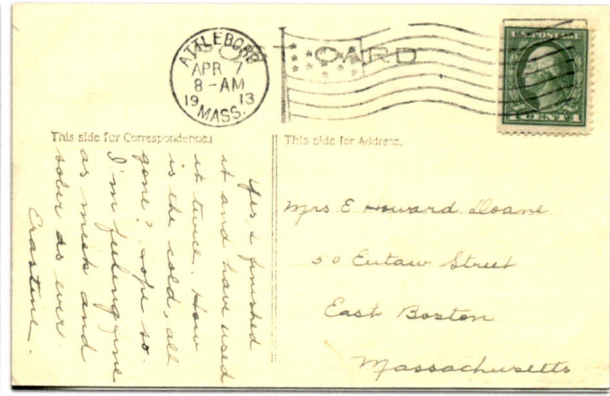

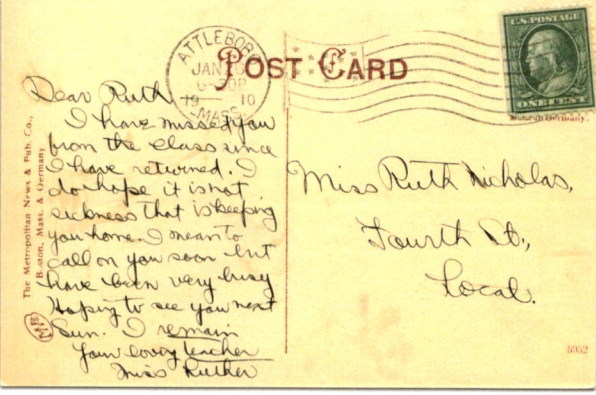

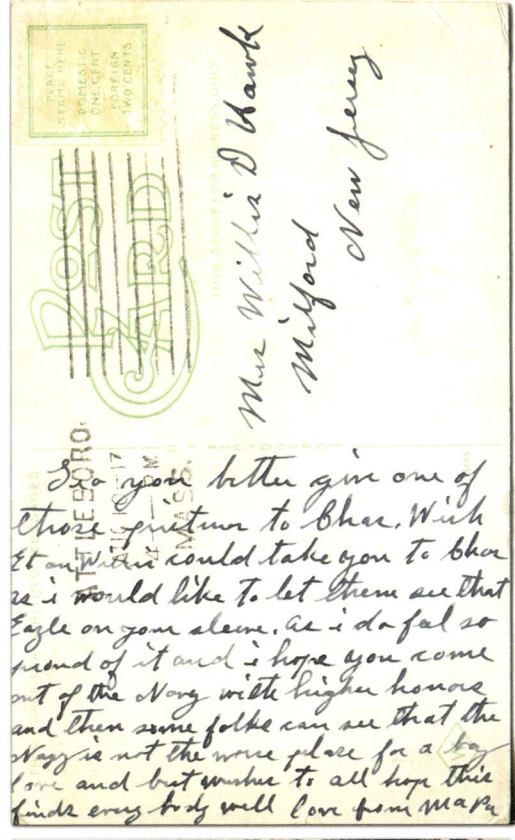

Decoding a 1917 Postcard: Attleboro and the U.S. Navy's Role in World War I

A handwritten postcard from August 10, 1917, offers a unique glimpse into the life of a U.S. Navy sailor during World War I. The letter, sent from a mother to her son, conveys both pride and hope, referencing the "Eagle on your sleeve." This insignia suggests that the son had achieved the rank of Petty Officer, a position of leadership and technical expertise in the Navy. The Petty Officer's rank featured an eagle perched atop chevrons, signifying responsibility and skill in the naval hierarchy. The mother's words also reflect a broader sentiment, attempting to reassure her son and others that the Navy was an honorable and valuable place to serve.

As the United States entered World War I in April 1917, Attleboro, Massachusetts, played a significant role in supporting the war effort. Known for its thriving jewelry and metalworking industries, the city was a key producer of military insignia, buttons, and decorations. Companies such as Evans & Co. and Balfour supplied the Navy with essential regalia, ensuring that enlisted men proudly wore their ranks

Beyond manufacturing, Attleboro also saw many of its young men enlist in the Navy. With a growing demand for sailors to combat German U-boat threats, the Navy expanded rapidly. Petty Officers, like the one referenced in the postcard, were instrumental in training new recruits, maintaining ship operations, and leading missions to safeguard convoys transporting American troops and supplies to Europe.

During World War I, the U.S. Navy played a crucial role in the war effort, particularly in anti-submarine warfare and convoy escort operations. The German navy posed a severe threat to Allied shipping, and the United States responded by deploying destroyers and battleships to protect merchant and troop transport vessels. Petty Officers held significant responsibilities in these operations, reinforcing discipline and efficiency onboard naval ships.

Public perception of naval service in 1917 was a mix of pride and apprehension. Many families, like the mother in the postcard, expressed deep pride in their loved ones' service but also harbored concerns about the dangers of U-boat attacks and combat at sea. However, the Navy was increasingly seen as an elite and respected branch of the military, essential to securing American and Allied interests overseas

The 1917 postcard is more than just a personal message—it is a reflection of the era's patriotic spirit, the evolving perception of naval service, and Attleboro's role in equipping and supplying the Navy. As Petty Officers took on leadership roles in the fleet, they carried with them the support of their families and communities, ensuring that their contributions would be remembered as part of both local and national history.

CBI Water Tower News. "Attleboro's Military Contributions." 1917, p. 7.

Daggett, John. Sketch of the History of Attleboro, 1800s. Press of Samuel Usher, 1894, p. 43, 85.

GREETINGS FROM ATTLEBORO

GREETINGS FROM ATTLEBORO

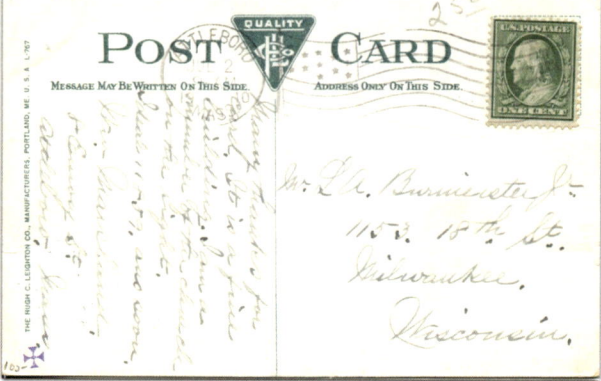

MONUMENTS OF ATTLEBORO

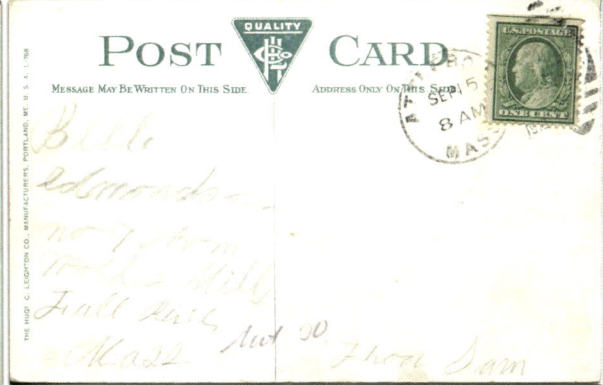

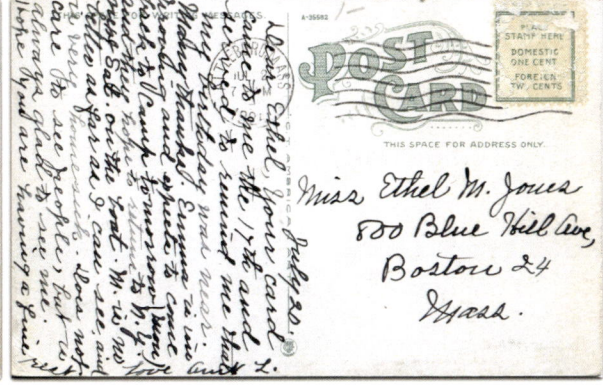

The War Monuments of Attleboro

Attleboro, Massachusetts, a city rich in historical heritage, has long honored its past through the preservation of its monuments. Among the city's most significant memorials are the Soldiers Monument, the D.A.R. Memorial Monument, and the Spanish War Monument, each reflecting the community's enduring respect for those who served in pivotal conflicts throughout American history.

The **Soldiers Monument**, a cornerstone of Attleboro's historical landscape, stands as a solemn tribute to local soldiers who served in the Civil War. Erected in the late 19th century, this monument is part of a national movement to memorialize the sacrifice of Union soldiers. Civil War service was extensive in Attleboro, as many men from the town enlisted to fight for the Union cause. Their names, along with the battles they fought in, are inscribed on the monument as a permanent testament to their bravery.

Such monuments were significant during the post-war reconstruction era, reinforcing a sense of unity and national pride. They also played an important role in shaping the narrative of the war, especially as veterans' organizations sought to preserve their experiences and contributions for future generations. Today, the Soldiers Monument stands as a reminder of the cost of preserving the Union and the community's commitment to honoring its past.

Located near the historic Old Peck House, **the D.A.R. Memorial Monument** was erected by the Daughters of the American Revolution (DAR) to honor the town's Revolutionary War veterans. The DAR has long been dedicated to preserving the memory of America's founding generation, and this monument reflects their mission to ensure that the sacrifices of early patriots are not forgotten.

The Old Peck House, now the DAR's local chapter house, serves as a living museum of Attleboro's colonial past. The monument itself is a focal point of the site, encouraging reflection on the contributions of Attleboro's Revolutionary War soldiers. It serves as a historical touchstone, connecting present-day residents to the city's 18th-century roots.

While less widely recognized than its Civil War counterpart, the **Spanish War Monument** commemorates Attleboro's role in the Spanish-American War of 1898. The war, which saw the United States emerge as a global power, was fought primarily in Cuba and the Philippines. The memorial, likely located within Capron Park, recognizes the local soldiers who answered the call to serve.

Capron Park itself was established in 1901 as a public space dedicated in memory of Dennis Capron, and over the years, it has become a site where various war monuments stand. Attleboro men who served in the Spanish-American War were part of a broader wave of young men who volunteered in a conflict driven by expansionist ideals and the call to liberate Spanish territories from colonial rule.

Attleboro's war monuments are more than just stone and inscriptions; they are active reminders of the sacrifices made by those who came before. Whether honoring the struggles of the Civil War, the patriots of the American Revolution, or the soldiers of the Spanish-American War, these memorials ensure that their legacies endure. As visitors walk past these monuments today, they stand in silent recognition of the courage and dedication that shaped both the city and the nation.

MONUMENTS OF ATTLEBORO

D.A.R. MEMORIAL MONUMENT, ATTLEBORO, MASS.

WAR MEMORIAL, ATTLEBORO, MASS.

Soldiers' Monument and Square, Attleboro, Mass.

Miscellaneous Attleboro

Additional Postcards from the Collection

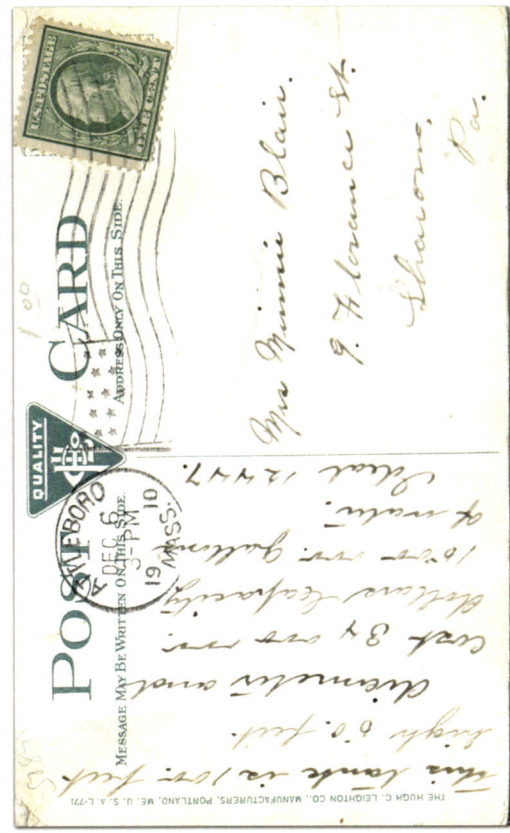

A Reinforced Concrete Marvel of Its Time

In the early 20th century, water infrastructure was rapidly evolving, and the Attleboro Standpipe stood at the forefront of innovation. Built in 1906, this reinforced concrete standpipe was hailed as the largest of its kind in the world. Measuring 100 feet high and 80 feet in diameter, the tank had a capacity of 1,000,000 gallons and cost $34,000 to construct. At a time when steel and wooden water towers were more common, Attleboro's choice to use reinforced concrete was both ambitious and experimental.

Standpipes like this were essential for municipal water systems, ensuring steady water pressure for residents and businesses while also providing a critical reserve for firefighting. While steel standpipes were widely used, concrete was gaining attention for its potential durability and cost-effectiveness. However, despite its initial promise, reinforced concrete standpipes often struggled with long-term structural integrity, a fate that likely befell the Attleboro tank.

Historical records from similar concrete standpipes built during this period highlight persistent issues with leakage and cracking. Engineers in the early 1900s were still refining their understanding of how water interacted with concrete over time, particularly in regions with freeze-thaw cycles like Massachusetts. In contrast, steel water tanks, pioneered by companies such as the Pittsburgh-Des Moines Steel Company and Chicago Bridge & Iron Works, became the preferred standard due to their superior water retention and longevity.

Other large standpipes from the same era—such as the Youngstown, Ohio standpipe (100 ft. diameter, 50 ft. high)—demonstrated similar challenges with reinforced concrete construction. By the 1920s and 1930s, improvements in pre-stressed concrete and steel fabrication led to the decline of early concrete standpipes.

While Attleboro's reinforced concrete standpipe was an impressive feat of engineering, it represented a transitional phase in water storage history. Its construction marked a bold step toward municipal innovation, yet its eventual decline mirrored the shift away from concrete tanks in favor of more durable steel alternatives.

Today, the legacy of Attleboro's standpipe remains an important part of the town's industrial history—one that reflects both ambition and the ever-evolving advancements in civil engineering.

Chicago Bridge and Iron Works. CBI Water Tower News. Chicago, 1914.

Dyal, Donald H. The Architecture of Water Towers: A Bibliography. Vance Bibliographies, 1982.

Garner, John S. "Tanks and Towers: Waterworks in America." American Public Architecture: European Roots and Native Expressions, edited by Craig Zabel and Susan Scott Munshower, Pennsylvania State University, 1989, pp. 184-228.

Pittsburgh-Des Moines Steel Company. Municipal Waterworks Bulletin. Pittsburgh, PA, 1924.

Dubie, R. A. Water Storage in America: 1850-1940. Journal of Civil Engineering History, 1980.

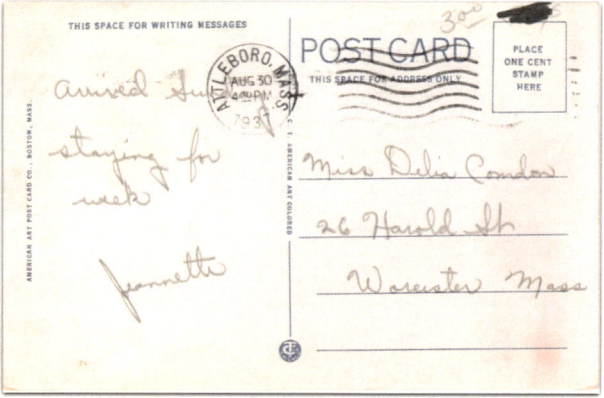

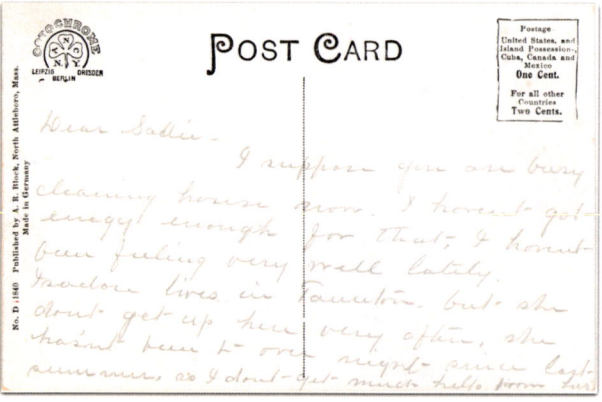

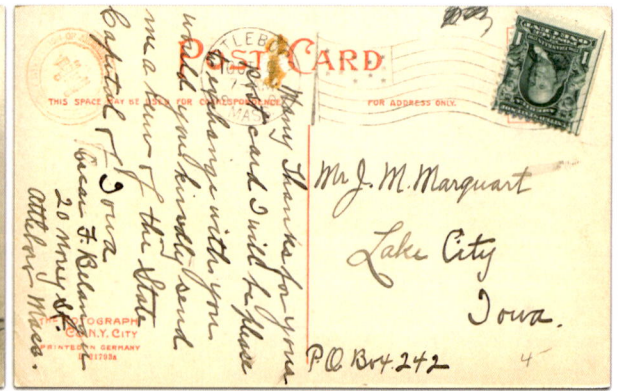

MISCELLANEOUS POSTCARDS

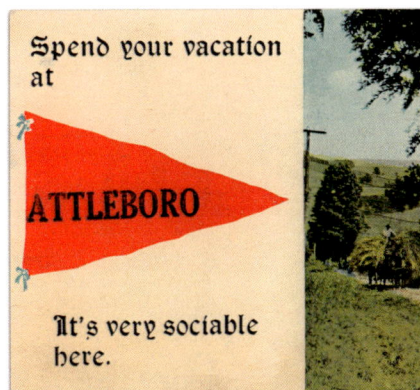

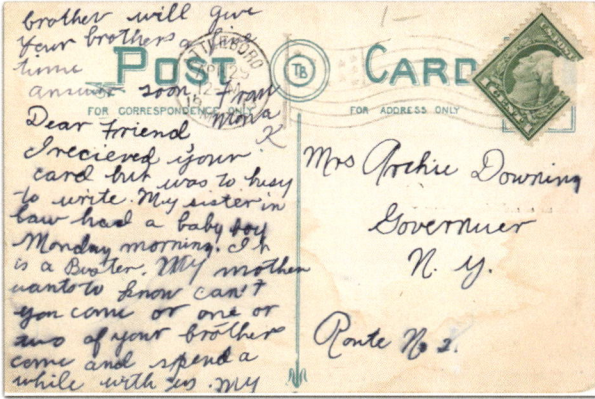

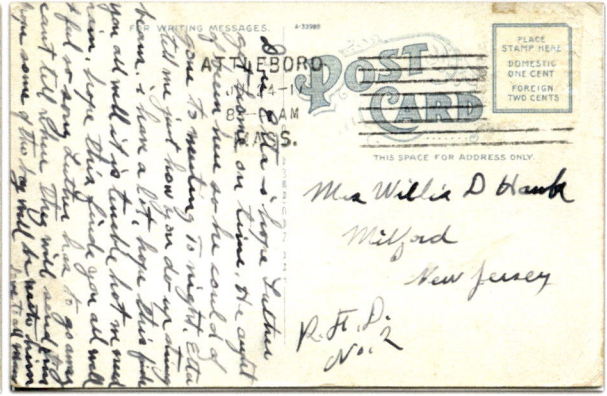

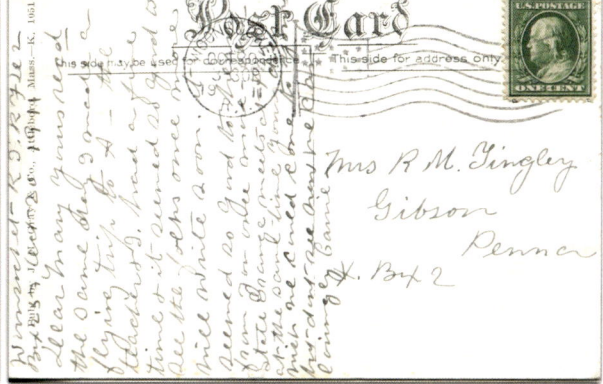

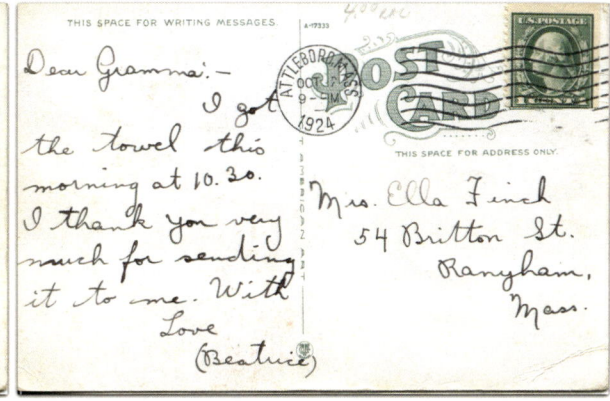

Hurricane Edna Sweeps Through New England: Attleboro Spared the Worst

On September 11, 1954, Hurricane Edna roared through New England, just days after Hurricane Carol had battered the region. The storm brought heavy rains, winds exceeding 100 mph, and widespread destruction. While parts of Massachusetts suffered major damage, reports from The Attleboro Sun indicate that Attleboro itself was relatively spared from the worst of the hurricane's wrath.

In the days leading up to Edna's arrival, emergency warnings were issued across New England, cautioning residents about gale-force winds and potential flooding. By September 10, preparations were in full swing. As Edna made landfall, Attleboro's police and fire departments were inundated with emergency calls, primarily concerning downed trees, power lines, and minor structural damage. According to the September 13 edition of The Attleboro Sun, multiple incidents occurred throughout the city, including fallen branches on power lines, a church steeple in danger of collapse, and reports of wires sparking against trees. Crews worked throughout the night to restore power and clear debris.

Despite the flurry of emergency calls, Attleboro did not experience the widespread destruction seen in other parts of New England. Statewide, the storm caused an estimated $500 million in damages, primarily in Massachusetts and Rhode Island. Flooding, tree damage, and agricultural losses were severe, with entire apple and peach crops destroyed. Insurance companies reported massive claims, while government officials scrambled to assess the total impact.

A personal account of the storm's aftermath is captured in a postcard sent on September 16, 1954, just days after the hurricane. Addressed to Thomas Sturtz in Johnstown, Pennsylvania, the writer describes a "quiet, restful time" but acknowledges the devastation around them, calling it "pathetic." The contrast between the official reports of destruction and the postcard's more personal reflection highlights the resilience of those who weathered the storm.

While Attleboro was fortunate to escape significant devastation, the storm serves as a reminder of nature's unpredictability. The community's quick response and the ability to carry on in the days following Edna reflect the strength of its residents during one of the most intense hurricane seasons in New England's history.

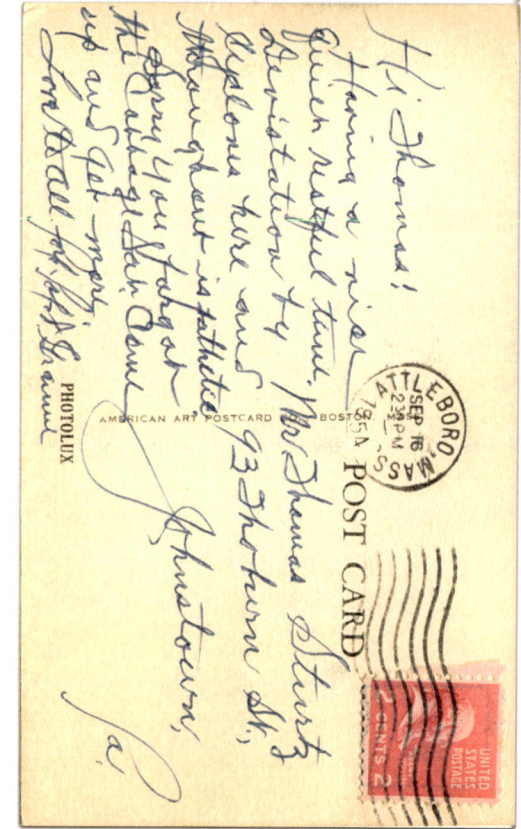

The Attleboro Sun. "EXTRA!! Hurricane Is Threat to City, Warning Says." The Attleboro Sun, 10 Sept. 1954, p. 2.

The Attleboro Sun. "Hurricanes May Have Dealt $500,000,000 Economic Blow to N.E." The Attleboro Sun, 13 Sept. 1954, p. 16.

The Attleboro Sun. "Police and Fire Dept. Logs Record Hurricane Calls." The Attleboro Sun, 14 Sept. 1954, p. 2.

MISCELLANEOUS POSTCARDS

The Great Temperature Plunge of March 1921: A Day of Weather Extremes

On March 28-29, 1921, the Northeast experienced one of the most extreme and abrupt weather shifts in recorded history. What began as a warm spring day with temperatures soaring to 78°F in some areas quickly turned into a winter storm, bringing snow, powerful winds, and record-breaking temperature drops across the region.

A postcard sent from Western Massachusetts captures the surreal nature of this event, *"We got your frost slightly and a thunder shower too. They followed your card! Western Mass. had 15 in. of snow and 78° all the same day."*

Indeed, this postcard reflects a reality that seemed impossible. On the morning of March 28, 1921, temperatures in New York City climbed from 49°F at 5 AM to a record-breaking 82°F by 2 PM. But within hours, a powerful cold front swept through, bringing violent winds, thunderstorms, and an unprecedented temperature drop. Between 4 PM and 5 PM, New York's temperature plunged 29°F—from 81°F to 52°F—marking the largest one-hour temperature drop in the city's history at the time. By midnight, the mercury had fallen to 34°F, and by 6 AM on March 29, it had bottomed out at 26°F.

Across the Northeast, this drastic shift played out in similar fashion. Western Massachusetts, particularly in the Berkshires, saw an even more shocking transformation. After basking in near 80-degree warmth, residents awoke to a full-blown winter storm dumping 15 inches of snow. Neighboring states, including New Jersey, Connecticut, and upstate New York, also reported record-breaking temperature swings.

The storm was not just a temperature anomaly; it brought intense winds, property damage, and even fatalities. In Brooklyn, a young girl lost her life when a wall collapsed under the hurricane-force gusts. Meanwhile, in Staten Island, over a thousand barrels of oil were tossed into the waters as gales ripped through.

The Great Temperature Plunge of March 1921 remained one of the most astonishing meteorological events in U.S. history for over a century—a day when summer turned to winter in a matter of hours. However, in December 2022, another extreme cold front surpassed this record, bringing an even greater 50-degree temperature drop in a single day. While the 1921 event stunned the Northeast with its rapid descent from 78°F to freezing temperatures, the 2022 Arctic blast reinforced how volatile and unpredictable weather patterns can be, even a century later.

Newman, Andy. "For a Hot-and-Cold March, 1921 Has 2011 Beat." The New York Times, 29 Mar. 2011, archive.nytimes.com.

"Today in New York Weather History: March 28." The Starry Eye Weather Blog, 28 Mar. 2013, thestarryeye.typepad.com.

Glen Allen Weather. "March Weather Events." Glen Allen Weather Historical Events, glenallenweather.com.

WeatherWeb. "Weather in History 1900 to 1949 AD." WeatherWeb Premium, premium.weatherweb.net.

"December 2022 Arctic Blast and Temperature Drop." NOAA National Weather Service, Dec. 2022, weather.gov.

GREETINGS FROM ATTLEBORO

View of Camp Hebron, Attleboro, Mass.

Farmer's Den, Attleboro, Mass. Pub. by S. P. Clark & Co.

Ten Mile River, Attleboro, Mass.

MISCELLANEOUS POSTCARDS

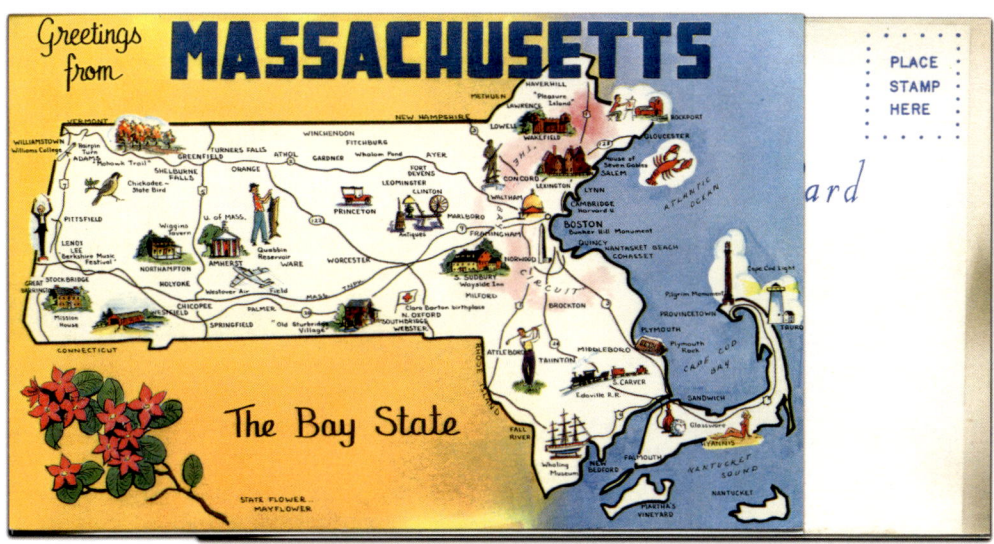

GREETINGS FROM ATTLEBORO

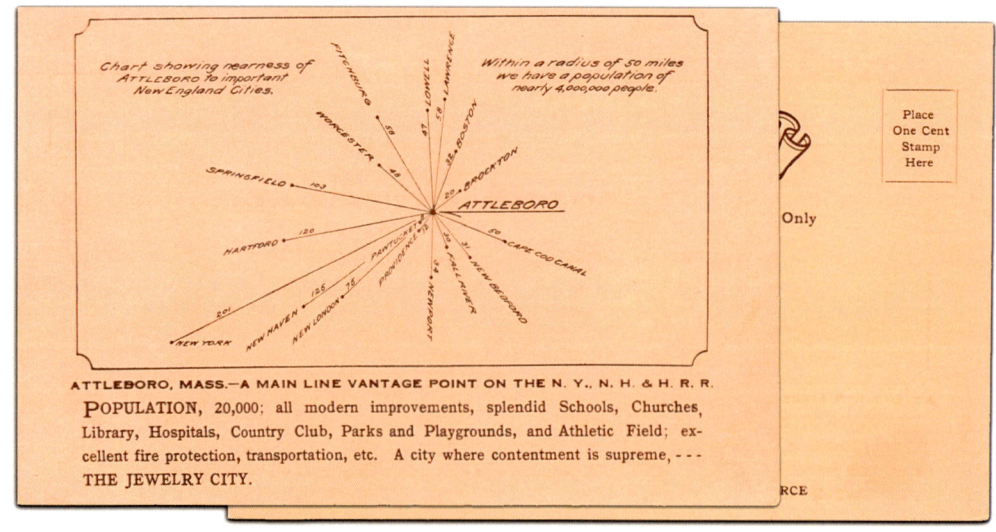

www.ingramcontent.com/pod-product-compliance
Lightning Source LLC
Chambersburg PA
CBRC091722070526
44585CB00008B/152